BROOKLYN DODGERS:

The Last Great Pennant Drive, 1957

The Last Great Pennant Drive, 1957

John R. Nordell, Jr.

✳ Tribute Books
Eynon, Pennsylvania

First Edition, May 2007
Copyright © 2007 by John R. Nordell, Jr.

Library of Congress Control Number: 2007924997

ISBN 978-0-9765072-9-1

Published in the United States by
❋ Tribute Books
291 West Street, Eynon, PA 18403
(570) 876-2416 • tribute-books.com
SAN #256-4416

Photo credits: Hy Peskin (*Time & Life* Pictures), p. 6.
Frank Hurley (*Daily News*/New York), pp. 49-50, 83.
Mark Kauffman (*Sports Illustrated*), Duke Snider, p. 67.
George Silk (*Time & Life* Pictures), Gil Hodges, p. 67.
Wil Blanche (*Sports Illustrated*), p. 78.
Alfred Eisenstaedt (*Time & Life* Pictures), p. 80.

Cover design: Nicole Langan
Cover photographs: (Top) Duke Snider
(Middle, L-R) Gil Hodges and Carl Furillo
(Bottom, L-R) Johnny Podres, Roy Campanella,
and Clem Labine.
Dodger logo and photos courtesy of the Los Angeles Dodgers.

Also By John R. Nordell, Jr.

The Undetected Enemy:
French and American Miscalculations
at Dien Bien Phu, 1953

To the Memory of
the Brooklyn Dodgers

Table of Contents

Preface

Nikita Khrushchev consolidated his power in the Soviet Union during a Kremlin showdown. The United States Senate was debating the first significant race legislation in decades that was given a serious chance of passage. The motion picture *Island in the Sun* was playing in theaters across America. And as major league baseball observed its annual All-Star game break, the defending National League champion Brooklyn Dodgers found themselves mired in fifth place.

It was July 1957.

That was my first year as a fan of the Brooklyn Dodgers. It was destined to be my last. The brevity of the experience and the enduring nature of childhood impressions may explain why my recollection of it remains so vivid a half century later. To this day, no baseball summer is as memorable for me as that July when the Dodgers began a winning streak in a suddenly torrid, topsy-turvy National League pennant race. It was also the month when I saw my first major league baseball game at Ebbets Field, which was the most exciting thing I had ever experienced.

This book describes a pivotal time during Brooklyn's last season in a baseball world now long gone. It was written for baseball lovers young and old but mainly for old Dodger fans who still recall these events and cherish their memories of them, as I do.

John R. Nordell, Jr.
Old Forge, Pennsylvania
February 24, 2007

Acknowledgments

This project was made all the more enjoyable by the friendly assistance of many people. I want to thank members of the reference departments at the Osterhout Free Library in Wilkes-Barre, Pennsylvania and the Albright Memorial Library in Scranton, Pennsylvania, where much of my research was done. The staff of the library at the National Baseball Hall of Fame in Cooperstown, New York provided invaluable guidance, especially Gabe Schechter. My thanks also to Warren Platt of the New York Public Library, Katherine LaBarbera and Jean E. M. Gosebrink of the St. Louis Public Library, and Claus Guglberger of the New York *Daily News*. For assistance with my photographs, I especially want to thank Gabe Dalessandro of the UPS Store in Edwardsville, Pennsylvania as well as Ed Menjak of Professional Photographic Services in Wilkes-Barre. I appreciate the permission that was granted by team historian Mark Langill to use photographs and other insignia of the Dodgers. I am grateful to David Smith for his instructions on using *www.retrosheet.org*, which is the best fact-checker that a researcher on baseball could ever have. It was a pleasure working with Nicole Langan of Tribute Books in pulling together the various elements of this book.

My deepest gratitude and love go to my family. My late parents, John and Dorothy Nordell, sparked my interest in baseball and my loyalty to the Brooklyn Dodgers. I will always remember my mother's encouragement and advice about the manuscript in its early stages. My wife Marianne assisted me on my research trips. Her companionship was a joy, as in all our endeavors.

Chapter 1

Homers and a Rhubarb

A ninth-inning rally by the National League fell one run short as the American League barely saved a 6-5 victory in the twenty-fourth All-Star game on Tuesday, July 9, 1957 at Busch Stadium in St. Louis. Starting pitcher Jim Bunning of the Detroit Tigers pitched three perfect innings to earn the American League victory. Detroit right fielder Al Kaline exhibited a golden glove on two outfield plays and also got two hits, driving in two runs. Chicago White Sox outfielder Minnie Minoso doubled home what proved to be the winning run in the top of the ninth and made a game-saving throw during the bottom of the ninth. Starter Curt Simmons of the Philadelphia Phillies took the loss.

The National Leaguers were managed by Walter Alston of the Brooklyn Dodgers, whose team had been in the previous year's World Series against Casey Stengel's New York Yankees. No Dodger players were in the starting lineup for the National All-Stars although first baseman Gil Hodges, outfielder Gino Cimoli, and relief pitcher Clem Labine saw action late in the game.

In the only game scheduled in the National League on Wednesday, July 10, the Pittsburgh Pirates defeated the Milwaukee Braves 5-2 at Forbes Field in Pittsburgh. The Pirates tied the game at 2-2 in the fourth inning when, with a runner on first, left fielder Bob Skinner hit an inside-the-park home run. Pirate third baseman Gene Baker supplied the payoff hit with a three-run single in the sixth to break the tie. Winning pitcher Bob Purkey, who gave up six hits

1

in going the distance, was 9-7 on the season. He went into
the game with a 2.76 earned run average, which was tops
in the National League. Losing pitcher Bob Buhl was
charged with his fifth defeat in fourteen decisions.

The outcome did not affect the Dodgers' fifth-place
position, five games out of first place. As the National
League prepared to resume a full schedule of games on the
following day, the pennant race shaped up as follows:

Standings	Won	Lost	Pct.	GB
St. Louis Cardinals	46	31	.597	-
Milwaukee Braves	44	35	.557	3
Philadelphia Phillies	42	34	.553	3 ½
Cincinnati Redlegs	44	36	.550	3 ½
Brooklyn Dodgers	41	36	.532	5
New York Giants	36	43	.456	11
Pittsburgh Pirates	30	49	.380	17
Chicago Cubs	26	45	.366	17

On Thursday, July 11, the Philadelphia Phillies took a
pair from the Chicago Cubs in a twilight-night doubleheader at Connie Mack Stadium in Philadelphia. The first
game involved extra-innings shutout ball with Harvey
Haddox pitching for Philadelphia and Bob Rush for
Chicago. Rush didn't yield a hit until the eighth inning.
Haddox, who allowed eight hits, struck out eight, and
walked none, opened the Phillies' half of the eleventh
inning with a single. Center fielder Richie Ashburn laid
down a bunt and beat it out for a hit. Chuck Harmon ran
for Haddox. Reliever Turk Lown took over from Rush and
gave up a game-winning single to second baseman Granny
Hamner that scored Harmon and clinched a 1-0
Philadelphia victory. Winner Haddox was 8-5. Rush, who
was charged with the loss, was 1-8.

The second game featured Philadelphia's rookie pitcher Jack Sanford in a 3-1 win over the Cubs. Sanford's blazing speed and excellent control enabled him to retire the first twenty-two Cubs who faced him. He lost a perfect game in the eighth inning on a broken-bat single by first baseman Dale Long. Sanford's eleventh victory against two defeats made him the top winner in the senior circuit and his eight strike outs raised his season total to 104, which also led the league. A two-run double by rookie left fielder Harry Anderson in the third inning and a home run by catcher Joe Lonnett in the seventh gave the Phillies their winning margin. Losing pitcher Don Elston was 2-1.

A pitchers' duel at the Polo Grounds in New York ended with a 1-0 victory by the New York Giants over the St. Louis Cardinals. The Giants' Johnny Antonelli pitched five-hit ball but saw his performance matched by the Cardinals' Lindy McDaniel who allowed only three hits in seven innings. One of those hits, however, was a sixth inning home run by New York's rookie catcher Valmy Thomas, which proved decisive. Winner Antonelli was 8-7, with two shutouts. Loser McDaniel was 8-5. The Giants' star center fielder Willie Mays failed to break his slump, going zero for three. He was hitless in his last twelve times at bat, with only one hit in his last twenty-one trips to the plate.

The Milwaukee Braves handily defeated the Pittsburgh Pirates 7-2. Shortstop Johnny Logan drove in three of Milwaukee's runs, two of them on a homer which climaxed a four-run rally in the fourth inning and another on a single in the eighth. Winning pitcher Bob Trowbridge was 3-1. He gave up twelve hits but the Pirates left eleven base runners stranded and committed six errors. Pittsburgh hurler Bob Friend was charged with the loss and was 6-10. The Braves lost the services of starting shortstop Felix Mantilla and center fielder Bill Bruton who were hurt when they collided trying to catch a looping fly ball into short center field in the first inning.

The Brooklyn Dodgers opened the second half of the season with an important home stand at Ebbets Field. The first three teams they were scheduled to host were above them in the standings. That night's game was against the fourth-place Cincinnati Redlegs.

In the second inning, Brooklyn's rookie pitcher Danny McDevitt gave up singles to left fielder Frank Robinson and catcher Smokey Burgess, followed by a walk to third baseman Don Hoak, which loaded the bases with one out. Shortstop Roy McMillan hit a hard drive off McDevitt's glove which the pitcher recovered and fired to catcher Roy Campanella in time for a force at the plate. Robinson slid in hard, however, and spilled Campanella, who lost the ball and his glove, giving the Redlegs a 1-0 lead.

In the fourth inning, second baseman Jim (Junior) Gilliam singled to right against Redleg pitcher Brooks Lawrence and center fielder Duke Snider blasted his seventeenth home run of the year off the girder at the base of the upper deck in center field. A walk to right fielder Elmer Valo and singles by left fielder Gino Cimoli and first baseman Gil Hodges made it a three-run inning, sending Lawrence to the showers.

In a foretaste of things to come, virtually the entire Redleg team stormed the field in the fifth inning to protest when first base umpire Augie Donatelli called Gilliam safe on a close play. Relief pitcher Raul Sanchez fielded a bunt but the Cuban rookie, in tagging Gilliam on the baseline, dropped the ball after the tag as he was knocked sprawling.

In the sixth inning, Redleg first baseman George Crowe beat out an infield hit to first when Hodges bobbled the ball and his throw to McDevitt was too late. Robinson then hit his fourteenth home run. Burgess doubled to right, chasing starter McDevitt, and advanced to third when Hoak grounded to second against reliever Clem Labine. Burgess scored on a deep sacrifice fly to center by McMillan, for a 4-3 Cincinnati lead.

Dodger third baseman Don Zimmer was tossed out of the game by umpire Donatelli in the bottom of the sixth when he and other Dodgers argued over Sanchez's abrupt pick-off move when he nailed Zimmer at first base after receiving a new ball. The Dodgers claimed that Sanchez wasn't on the rubber and that time was out due to the insertion of a new ball. Donatelli insisted that Sanchez was on the rubber.

In the seventh inning, Gilliam hit the dirt ducking a head high pitch by Sanchez. On the next pitch, Gilliam attempted a drag bunt which hopped foul. As Gilliam ran toward first base, Sanchez rushed off the mound to field the ball. They collided on the baseline and Gilliam tore into the righthander. Punches flew between them as they went down, arms and legs flailing, with Gilliam landing on top. First baseman Crowe, who was already moving toward the baseline in response to Gilliam's bunt, was the first on the scene and threw himself on Gilliam. Campanella arrived from the Dodger dugout and pulled Crowe off Gilliam then Dodger manager Walter Alston grabbed Crowe from behind the shoulders and pulled him away. Hoak arrived from third base almost simultaneously with Dodger shortstop Charley Neal and was immediately felled by a right-hand punch from Neal, who bypassed the fight to get at Hoak. They struggled before Neal disappeared among the players from each club who joined the melee from field and dugout. Some squared off in side fights or confrontations, among them Crowe and Dodger Carl Furillo. Meanwhile, Redleg right fielder Pete Whisenant pulled Gilliam off Sanchez. The brawl lasted for almost fifteen minutes, with the crowd in an uproar.[1]

(Above) Raul Sanchez (32) and Jim Gilliam (19) collide,
Gilliam attacks, and the two players struggle.

(Below) Roy Campanella pulls George Crowe off Gilliam as
coach Jake Pitler (top), Smokey Burgess (bottom), Don
Hoak (left), and Charley Neal (right) arrive on the scene.

Source: *Sports Illustrated.*

As things were starting to quiet down, Hoak, an ex-Dodger, suddenly charged the Dodger dugout. Hoak had said what he would like to do to Neal and Neal, standing on the steps of the dugout, had invited Hoak to come and do it. Hodges stopped Hoak and Neal was hustled away by teammates. Hoak was then escorted from the field and, along with Gilliam, Sanchez, and Neal, was thrown out of the game.

Cincinnati manager Birdie Tebbetts, at the apparent direction of chief umpire Jocko Conlan, kept Hoak on the bench to prevent the third baseman from seeking to continue the fight under the stands in the players' runway. Hoak later claimed he was hit from behind and termed Neal's blow a "sucker punch."[2] When interviewed, he said: "I actually went in there to stop the fight [between Gilliam and Sanchez] and out of a clear sky I was hit."[3] When it was suggested to Hoak that he would be calmed down by the following day's game with the Dodgers, he replied: "I will not. I'm going to get him [Neal] either inside or outside the ball park."[4]

When play finally resumed,[5] rookie Johnny Roseboro, batting for Gilliam, walked against new Redleg pitcher Tom Acker, who replaced Sanchez. Snider then reached the lower left-center field seats with his second two-run homer of the game, which put Brooklyn ahead for good, 5-4. Snider's eighteen home runs were the third highest in the National League. Hank Aaron of the Milwaukee Braves had twenty-seven and Stan Musial of the St. Louis Cardinals had twenty. Seventh-inning reliever Roger Craig got the win and was 4-5. Acker took the loss and was 9-4.

The Dodgers were now four games out of first place.

Standings	Won	Lost	Pct.	GB
St. Louis Cardinals	46	32	.590	-
Philadelphia Phillies	44	34	.564	2
Milwaukee Braves	45	35	.563	2
Cincinnati Redlegs	44	37	.543	3 ½
Brooklyn Dodgers	42	36	.538	4
New York Giants	37	43	.463	10
Pittsburgh Pirates	30	50	.375	17
Chicago Cubs	26	47	.356	17 ½

On Friday, July 12, the Milwaukee Braves edged the Pittsburgh Pirates 5-4 as rookie relief pitcher Don McMahon squelched a two-run rally by the Pirates in the ninth inning. Starter Warren Spahn and Pirate pitcher Vernon Law were engaged in a scoreless duel until the sixth inning when Milwaukee center fielder Hank Aaron connected for his twenty-eighth home run. The Braves added another run that inning and one in the seventh, to take a 3-2 lead. Johnny Logan led off the ninth for Milwaukee with a homer. An error by Pirate first baseman Dee Fondy on a grounder by third baseman Eddie Mathews set the stage for the decisive fifth run when Mathews went to third on a single by left fielder Wes Covington and scored on an infield out by first baseman Frank Torre. Spahn earned his ninth victory against seven defeats. Pirate relief pitcher Elroy Face took the loss and was 3-5.

The Chicago Cubs scored a 5-2 victory over the Philadelphia Phillies on the strength of home runs by rookie third baseman Jerry Kindall and shortstop Ernie Banks. Kindall homered to lead off for the Cubs in the first inning and hit a two-run blast in the ninth. Banks unloaded a two-run homer, his sixteenth, in the eighth inning. Phillie pitcher Robin Roberts allowed eleven hits, struck out nine, and walked one before leaving the game, tagged with his twelfth loss against six wins. The three Cub home runs gave Roberts a National League leading total of twenty-six home runs given up. The defeat also marked the first time in Roberts' career that the once great righthander lost six games in a row. Cub reliever Jim Brosnan gained his first victory against two defeats.

The St. Louis Cardinals defeated the New York Giants 5-1 as first baseman Stan Musial hit his twenty-first home run. Shortstop Alvin Dark and second baseman Don Blasingame also slugged round-trippers. Pitcher "Toothpick" Sam Jones had a no-hitter going until the sixth inning when Giant left fielder Whitey Lockman rifled a single off his glove. Willie Mays ended his hitless string at fifteen on his fourth trip to the plate in the ninth when he connected for his fourteenth home run, his first in two weeks, which produced New York's only run. The game was held up in the fifth when Giant pitcher Ruben Gomez threw a bean ball at Jones and umpire Tom Gorman warned Gomez and Jones and their respective managers, Bill Rigney of the Giants and Fred Hutchinson of the Cards, against this practice. Both pitchers had tossed "dusters" at each other in the third. Winning pitcher Jones yielded two hits and struck out eight in collecting his seventh victory against three defeats. Loser Gomez was 10-6.

That day National League President Warren Giles wired the following warning to Don Hoak from his office in Cincinnati:

> You are quoted in the morning paper here as saying you "will get him in the ball park or outside." The "him," no doubt, refers to Neal. I do not have the umpire's report of the incident at Brooklyn last night and will deal with it when I have that report. In view

of the quotation in the morning paper,
however, I feel impelled to advise you that
any revival of the incident, whether it be on
the field or off the field, will be considered
a serious offense and dealt with accordingly.
You owe it to yourself and your club not to
revive the incident.[6]

Later that day Giles sent the following telegram to
Hoak, Jim Gilliam, Charley Neal, and Raul Sanchez:

For your part in the melee at Ebbets Field,
Brooklyn, last night you are fined the sum
of $100, payable at [the] league office prior
to game time, July 17. Such actions are not
a part of the game, are not helpful to what
the game stands for and are not to be engaged
in. Any revival of the affair or repetition will
be dealt with more severely.[7]

That evening the Dodgers and the Redlegs faced one
another again, playing at Roosevelt Stadium in Jersey City,
New Jersey instead of Ebbets Field.[8] Gilliam and Neal
were in the lineup for Brooklyn but Hoak was replaced at
third base by Alex Grammas for Cincinnati. Hoak had sus-
tained two bruised and swollen fingers in the rhubarb and
found that he couldn't swing the bat properly in batting
practice.

Gil Hodges opened the second inning for the Dodgers
with a drive to deep left-center field off pitcher Johnny
Klippstein that was misjudged by Redleg center fielder
Gus Bell and rolled for a triple. Roy Campanella brought
Hodges home with a sacrifice fly.

George Crowe led off the Cincinnati seventh with a line
single to right against pitcher Don Newcombe. Crowe

(Top left) Duke Snider was a powerful hitter, a great defensive center fielder, and he ranked third in the league in home runs.

(Top right) Don Newcombe's nine victories lead the Dodger pitching staff and gave him a shot at a twenty-game season.

(Bottom left) Gino Cimoli's crackling batting average showed why he became an All-Star and a full-time Dodger outfielder.

(Bottom right) Manager Walter Alston tended to the details of leadership and was in his fourth year at Brooklyn's helm.

Sources: (Top and bottom right) Dodger photos; (bottom left) 1958 Dodger yearbook.

stopped at second on catcher Ed Bailey's looping single to left-center field and both runners advanced on Pete Whisenant's sacrifice bunt. Crowe then scored on a grounder to short by Grammas to tie the game at 1-1.

Gilliam opened the eighth inning for Brooklyn with a walk and went to third on left fielder Elmer Valo's single to right. Bob Kennedy ran for Valo. Right fielder Gino Cimoli then lined a 3-0 pitch to right-center for a triple that scored two runs for a 3-1 Dodger lead, which proved decisive.

Winning pitcher Newcombe allowed five singles, walked none, struck out seven, and retired sixteen Redlegs in a row at one point. The big righthander was 9-6. Losing pitcher Klippstein was 3-9.

The Dodgers remained four games out of first place but moved from fifth place to fourth in the standings.

Standings	Won	Lost	Pct.	GB
St. Louis Cardinals	47	32	.595	-
Milwaukee Braves	46	35	.568	2
Philadelphia Phillies	44	35	.557	3
Brooklyn Dodgers	43	36	.544	4
Cincinnati Redlegs	44	38	.537	4 ½
New York Giants	37	44	.457	11
Chicago Cubs	27	47	.365	17 ½
Pittsburgh Pirates	30	51	.370	18

Notes to Chapter 1

1. Both Gilliam and Sanchez were seen as spoiling for a fight. In an article entitled "A Beef Grows in Brooklyn," *Sports Illustrated* wrote: "Cincinnati pitcher Raul Sanchez . . . sent Dodger Junior Gilliam sprawling with a duster on his second pitch. Gilliam, fuming, then bunted a pop foul down the first-base line. Though there was no chance for a play, Sanchez charged after the ball and the pair met, as if by design, halfway between home and first." (*Sports Illustrated*, July 22, 1957, p. 22.) In the caption to a photograph accompanying the article, *Sports Illustrated* added: "Colliding as planned, Gilliam elbows Sanchez" (ibid., p. 21). In an article for *Street and Smith's 1958 Baseball Yearbook*, reporter Roscoe McGowen wrote that the fight "was instigated by Jim Gilliam" (*Street and Smith's 1958 Baseball Yearbook*, p. 48). The caption to a photograph accompanying the article read: "Junior Gilliam lands on Red's Raul Sanchez after deliberate bunt as trap" (ibid., p. 49). In *The Sporting News*, however, McGowen wrote: "[A] sidelight, gleaned from my friend, Buck Canel, the bilingual broadcaster, concerns Sanchez. Raul doesn't speak English to any extent but expresses himself volubly in Spanish. 'I knew that bunt was going foul,' he told Buck. 'But I was going over there anyway'." (*The Sporting News*, July 24, 1957, p. 8.) Bad blood between Sanchez and the Dodgers began during a game in Cincinnati on June 18 when the righthander hit Neal in the back with one pitch and knocked Campanella down with two others.

2. *The Sporting News*, July 24, 1957, p. 7.

3. *The New York Times*, July 12, 1957, p. 24.

4. Ibid.

5. I watched this game on television and recall that immediately following the brawl, the partisan Brooklyn
crowd reacted to every ball or strike by booing or cheering. My attitude was similar at the time. I later under-
stood the culpability of Jim Gilliam and Charley Neal in
this incident, especially Neal, whose attack on Don
Hoak made an already violent situation even worse and
this ultimately overshadowed the original scrap between
Gilliam and Sanchez.

6. *The Sporting News*, July 24, 1957, p. 7.

7. Ibid.

8. On December 8, 1955, two months after Brooklyn
became World Champions, the Dodger organization
announced that beginning in 1956 the Dodgers would
play seven of their seventy-seven home games at
Roosevelt Stadium, with one game scheduled against
each of the other seven National League teams.

Chapter 2

A Squeaker and a Slaughter

On Saturday, July 13, the league-leading St. Louis Cardinals jumped to a 3-0 lead over the New York Giants in the first inning on the strength of a two-run single by left fielder Wally Moon and a one-run single by center fielder Ken Boyer off pitcher Curt Barclay. The Redbirds had just added an additional run in the second inning with a home run by Alvin Dark when, with two out, plate umpire Ken Burkhart called time when the rain that had been falling at the Polo Grounds since the first inning became too heavy to allow a continuation of the game. Baseball law dictated that umpires wait a minimum of thirty minutes before calling off a game because of inclement weather. Burkhart waited seventy-three minutes before finally bowing to the elements and nullifying everything that had happened.

While the teams were waiting for Burkhart's decision, word reached the Polo Grounds that the Milwaukee Braves had gained a 4-3 victory over the Pittsburgh Pirates. The Braves took the lead in the second inning with an inside-the-park home run by Wes Covington and added another run in the fourth. A two-run homer by catcher Del Crandall in the seventh inning gave the Braves a 4-1 lead and allowed them to survive a two-run rally by the Pirates in the ninth. Winning pitcher Lew Burdette scattered ten hits and earned his seventh victory of the season against six losses. He also belted what would have been a triple in the seventh inning but this was negated by his failure to touch first base. Losing pitcher Ronnie Kline was 2-12.

The number one and number three hitters in the National
League extended their hitting streaks. Hank Aaron of the
Braves, with a .348 batting average, had now hit safely in
fourteen games. Dee Fondy of the Pirates, with a .339
average, lengthened his streak to twelve games.[1]

The Philadelphia Phillies defeated the Chicago Cubs
5-2 in a game that starred Harry Anderson. The left fielder
got three hits in four trips to the plate, drove in three of
Philadelphia's runs, and connected for a two-run, inside-
the-park home run in the fifth inning. Joe Lonnett also
homered for the Phillies in the sixth. Winning pitcher
Warren Hacker, who allowed five hits in eight innings, was
5-2. The Cubs threatened in the ninth with two hits off
Hacker but rookie reliever Dick Farrell retired the side and
held the victory. Loser Dick Drott was 8-8.

Game three between the Brooklyn Dodgers and the
Cincinnati Redlegs returned to Ebbets Fields. Charley
Neal opened the first inning with a single off Cincinnati
pitcher Hal Jeffcoat and made it to third on a single by Jim
Gilliam. A walk to Duke Snider loaded the bases. Elmer
Valo sent a grounder to second baseman Johnny Temple
who flipped it too high to shortstop Roy McMillan to get a
force. Neal scored and the bases remained filled. A walk
to Gino Cimoli brought Gilliam across with another run
and produced a 2-0 lead. Gil Hodges hit a liner to Alex
Grammas, who stepped on third base for a double play and
almost made it a triple killing with his throw to George
Crowe at first, but Cimoli made it back just in time. The
inning ended without further scoring.

The Redlegs filled the bases with one out in the second
inning on three walks by pitcher Roger Craig. On the third
walk, to McMillan, the Dodgers contended that Craig had
thrown a perfect pitch, not ball four, and that Roy
Campanella's throw to third baseman Randy Jackson had

completed a double play on Redleg right fielder Jerry Lynch, who was running on a three-two pitch. Umpire Vic Delmore, who was calling the balls and strikes, became the target of Dodger protests. Delmore went to the Dodger bench to issue a warning but no one was banished. Reliever Ed Roebuck took over to end the inning by striking out Jeffcoat and getting Temple to hit a forcing grounder.

Third baseman Jackson, playing his first game since injuring his left knee on April 26 in Pittsburgh, led off the Dodger second inning with a line single to center field. With a count of one ball and two strikes on Roebuck, the game was halted by umpire Delmore. The same rain that had stopped play across town that day at the Polo Grounds was now falling more briskly. After waiting for forty minutes, the umpires looked at the skies and the condition of the field and decided to call the whole thing off. Lost from the records was Gilliam's single which would have extended his hitting streak to thirteen games.

Roscoe McGowen highlighted the role that Dodger pitching was playing that season:

> Seven different Dodger pitchers have an earned run mark of 3.00 or better. Danny McDevitt leads with 1.60 and [Sal] Maglie is next with 2.37. The others are Sandy Koafax, Johnny Podres, [Don] Newcombe, Clem Labine and Carl Erskine. Carl's mark is 3.00.[2]

With the washout of that day's game, the Dodgers remained four games out of first place.

Standings	Won	Lost	Pct.	GB
St. Louis Cardinals	47	32	.595	-
Milwaukee Braves	47	35	.573	1 ½
Philadelphia Phillies	45	35	.563	2 ½
Brooklyn Dodgers	43	36	.544	4
Cincinnati Redlegs	44	38	.537	4 ½
New York Giants	37	44	.457	11
Pittsburgh Pirates	30	52	.366	18 ½
Chicago Cubs	27	48	.360	18

On Sunday, July 14, the Philadelphia Phillies swept a doubleheader from the St. Louis Cardinals in Philadelphia. A three-run homer by right fielder Rip Republski in the first inning and a two-run double by pitcher Curt Simmons in the fourth chased eighteen-year-old bonus baby Von McDaniel, the younger brother of pitcher and fellow Cardinal Lindy McDaniel. Philadelphia scored a final run on a homer by first baseman Eddie Bouchee in the fifth inning to give them a 6-2 victory. Simmons pitched seven-hit ball and recorded his ninth victory in thirteen decisions. Loser McDaniel was 4-1.

In the nightcap, Philadelphia scored a run without a hit in the first inning then took a 3-0 lead in the second inning on back-to-back home runs by Joe Lonnett and shortstop Chico Fernandez, who hit an inside-the-parker. After St. Louis tied the game with one run in the second inning and two runs in the third, Philadelphia broke the game wide open in a four-run, four-hit third inning which saw nine men come to bat and the early exit of starting pitcher Larry Jackson. Bouchee hit his second homer of the day in the fourth inning and the Phillies went on to win 11-4, with twelve hits. The Cardinals had eleven hits of their own but winning pitcher Jim Hearn kept them well scattered to earn his fourth win against one defeat. Loser Jackson was 10-5.

In another doubleheader, the Cincinnati Redlegs took
two from the Pittsburgh Pirates in Pittsburgh, with big
innings figuring prominently in both contests. In the first
game, the Pirates scored five runs in the fifth inning and
were leading 6-3 after six innings but the Redlegs came
back to score six runs in the seventh, getting three singles
off starter Bob Purkey and five more off reliever Bob
Friend, to go ahead and eventually win 9-6. The fourth
Redleg hurler, Hershell Freeman, earned the victory and
was 4-1. Friend drew the loss and was 6-11.

In the second game, a five-run outburst by Cincinnati
in the first inning chased Pittsburgh starter Joe Trimble and
an additional run in the second inning was followed by
back-to-back home runs by first baseman Ted Kluszewski
and Smokey Burgess in the fourth, for an 8-0 lead. Big
Klu smacked another homer in the sixth inning and the
Redlegs added three runs in the ninth, for a 12-4 victory.
Winning pitcher Joe Nuxhall went the distance for his third
victory in eight decisions. Loser Trimble was 0-2. There
were a total of fifty-five hits in the two contests: fourteen
by Cincinnati in the first game and nineteen in the second;
twelve hits by Pittsburgh in the first game and ten in the
second. None of the hits in the second game, however,
was by Dee Fondy, thus ending the Pirate first baseman's
hitting streak at thirteen games.

The New York Giants defeated the Chicago Cubs 8-6 in
an extra innings contest in New York in which both sides
used four pitchers. The Giants got off to 2-0 lead in the
first inning with home runs by Whitey Lockman and left
fielder Bobby Thomson. Chicago took a 4-2 lead in the
fourth inning but New York came back twice to tie the
game, at 4-4 in the fourth inning and at 6-6 in the ninth,
the latter on Lockman's second homer of the day. The
Cubs loaded the bases in the twelfth inning, with right
fielder Walt Moryn hitting his fifth single of the game, but

were unable to score. In the Giant half of the twelfth, a two-run homer by Willie Mays, his fifteenth of the season, won the game. Winning pitcher Marv Grissom was 2-2. Loser Jim Brosnan was 1-3.

The Milwaukee Braves came to Brooklyn on July 14 for a two-game set. The first batter to face Dodger pitcher Sal "The Barber" Maglie[3] was second baseman Red Schoendienst who, on a 2-1 pitch, knocked the ball over the right field screen, putting Milwaukee ahead 1-0. Hank Aaron singled, extending his hitting streak to fifteen games, but he was left on base.

In the Brooklyn half of the first, Charley Neal lined a double into the left field corner off pitcher Bob Buhl, moved to third on a sacrifice fly to right by Jim Gilliam,[4] then tagged and headed for home when third baseman Eddie Mathews, running hard, caught Duke Snider's high pop foul near the left field stands. Neal beat Mathews' throw to the plate, tying the game at 1-1.

The Maglie-Buhl duel continued for the next six innings, with both men beating back occasional threats. Johnny Podres took over on the mound for the Dodgers in the top of the eighth after Maglie was replaced by a pinch-hitter in the seventh.

With two out in the Milwaukee ninth, Frank Torre came to the plate. He had twice doubled to right field, off the wall in the second inning and off the scoreboard in the fourth, but was stranded on second base both times. Torre now hit one inside the first base line that rolled for his third right field double. Lew Burdette was sent in to run for him. Right fielder Andy Pafko hit a shot to left-center field that became an automatic ground rule double when it was caught by a fan below the top of the wall. Burdette scored and the Braves went ahead 2-1.

The first batter in the bottom of the ninth, Gino Cimoli,

drew a walk. On Buhl's first pitch to Gil Hodges, the first baseman hit a deep drive that landed eight rows back in the lower left-center field stands for his eleventh home run and first since June 26, giving Brooklyn an out-of-the-blue 3-2 victory. "Well, if you're going to win 'em, I guess that's the way to do it," proclaimed Dodger announcer Al Helfer.[5] A welcoming delegation of virtually every Dodger, including manager Walter Alston, greeted Hodges at home plate.[6] No one was wearing a wider grin than Podres who got the win, his first ever against the Braves, and was 7-3. Losing pitcher Buhl was 9-6.

The Dodgers were now two-and-a-half games out of first place.

Standings	Won	Lost	Pct.	GB
St. Louis Cardinals	47	34	.580	-
Philadelphia Phillies	47	35	.573	½
Milwaukee Braves	47	36	.566	1
Brooklyn Dodgers	44	36	.550	2 ½
Cincinnati Redlegs	46	38	.548	2 ½
New York Giants	38	44	.463	9 ½
Pittsburgh Pirates	30	54	.357	18 ½
Chicago Cubs	27	49	.355	17 ½

The list of superlatives used to describe the National League pennant race grew on Monday, July 15, when the new issue of *Sports Illustrated* called it "white-hot."[7] In recent days the Associated Press had referred to the five-contender race as "exciting"[8] and "dizzy."[9] It stood in marked contrast to the situation in the American League where the first-place New York Yankees faced serious competition from just one team, the Chicago White Sox, who were three games behind. The third-place Boston Red Sox trailed the Bronx Bombers by eleven games.

Both *Time* and *Newsweek* carried articles in their latest issues on the importance of good pitching in the National League pennant race, especially for the St. Louis Cardinals.

Wrote *Time*:

> All season long, the mercurial league lead has gone to the team best able to patch up its fundamental flaws (the Phillies cannot hit; the Redlegs are weak in pitching; the Dodgers are getting old; the Braves are injury-prone). . . . In St. Louis, fans are betting already that the fast balls of [Larry] Jackson and [Sam] Jones and the two kid pitchers from Oklahoma [Von and Lindy McDaniel] have turned the Cardinals into the one solid team in the pennant scramble.[10]

Observed *Newsweek*:

> The league-leading St. Louis Cardinals, Stan Musial aside, were up there largely because of the smooth, smart pitching they were getting from their youngsters: Lindy McDaniel, 21; his brother Von, 18; and Larry Jackson, 25. Fire-baller Jack Sanford, 27, is the key to the surprising surge of the Phillies, and elsewhere in the National League batters were swinging futilely at the amazing combinations of speed and change-ups fired by Chicago's Dick Drott, 21, and Brooklyn's Danny McDevitt, 24, and Don Drysdale, 21.[11]

(Top left) First baseman Gil Hodges was a consistently great hitter and always a home run threat, especially in the clutch.

(Top right) Catcher Roy Campanella was steady behind the plate, had a powerful bat, and was a dogged competitor.

(Bottom left) Southpaw Johnny Podres was having his best year on the mound and he finally beat the Milwaukee Braves.

(Bottom right) Forty-year-old Sal Maglie used his pitching cunning to win games and become Brooklyn's old pro hurler.

Source: Dodger photos.

In Philadelphia that day, Jack Sanford pitched the Phillies to a 6-2 victory over the St. Louis Cardinals, garnering his twelfth win against two defeats. The righthander yielded only five hits, fanned seven batters, and continued to lead the National League in strikeouts and victories. Philadelphia took the lead in the second inning when third baseman Willie Jones hit a two-run homer. A four-run rally by the Phillies in the third chased St. Louis starter Wilmer "Vinegar Bend" Mizell[12] and the Cardinals could only muster two runs thereafter. Loser Mizell was 3-7.

Willie Mays led the New York Giants to a 5-3 win over the Chicago Cubs as he continued his resurgence from the worst batting slump of his career. He hit his sixteenth home run, his third in three games, along with a run-producing double, and stole his twenty-fourth base. New York took a 1-0 lead in the second inning on right fielder Don Mueller's home run. Mays' two-run homer capped a three-run Giant rally in the fourth inning and he scored their final run in the eighth after he doubled, moved to third on a bunt, and came home on a sacrifice fly. Winning pitcher Johnny Antonelli survived a three-run Cub rally in the fourth but he needed help in the eighth from reliever Al Worthington to notch his ninth victory against seven defeats. Loser Don Elston was 2-2.

The Cincinnati Redlegs and the Pittsburgh Pirates were not scheduled.

The final game between the Brooklyn Dodgers and the Milwaukee Braves was played that night. In the bottom of the first inning, Charley Neal hit a home run off pitcher Bob Trowbridge and Milwaukee tied it 1-1 in the top of the second on a homer by catcher Carl Sawatski against pitcher Don Drysdale.

In the bottom of the second, Roy Campanella walked,

moved to third on a single to right by Randy Jackson, and scored on a grounder to third by Drysdale, giving the Dodgers a 2-1 lead.

In the third inning, Jim Gilliam singled to left and Duke Snider knocked a towering fly that was helped by the wind over the scoreboard for his nineteenth home run. Left fielder Sandy Amoros also homered, putting Brooklyn ahead 5-1. Roy Campanella walked, sending Trowbridge to the showers. Reliever Ernie Johnson ended the inning.

In the fourth inning, Drysdale helped his cause by hitting a home run. He was followed by Neal who hit his second homer of the game. Gilliam singled to center, chasing Johnson, who was replaced by Gene Conley. Snider rapped a single to right, with Gilliam going to third and Snider taking an extra base on the throw. Gino Cimoli walked, to load the bases. Gil Hodges hit a sacrifice fly to right, scoring Gilliam and moving Snider to third. Amoros forced Cimoli at second but Snider scored with the fourth run of the inning, for a 9-1 Brooklyn lead.

In the top of the sixth, Wes Covington singled to right and scored on a double to left by Frank Torre, making the score 9-2.

In the top of the seventh, Del Crandall, pinch-hitting for Conley, singled to left and scored the Braves' third run of the game on a double to right by Red Schoendienst, at which point Drysdale, who had given up nine hits, was relieved by Ed Roebuck.

In the home half of the seventh, new reliever Dave Jolly walked Hodges, who scored when Amoros doubled to right. Amoros, in turn, scored when Jackson doubled to right, putting the Dodgers ahead 11-3.

Covington hit a home run for Milwaukee in the eighth inning to make it 11-4.

Reliever Taylor Phillips, the Braves' fifth pitcher, took the mound against Brooklyn in the bottom of the eighth.

Could the Brooklyn Bums become the National League champions for the third year in a row in 1957?

Gilliam smashed an infield hit off third baseman Dick
Cole, who had replaced Eddie Mathews in the fifth. After
Snider looked at a third strike, Cimoli walked then Hodges
singled to right, scoring Gilliam. Cimoli made it to third
and Hodges to second on an error by right fielder Hank
Aaron. Amoros walked, loading the bases. Campanella
was hit on the foot by a pitch, forcing in Cimoli. Johnny
Roseboro ran for Campanella. Jackson hit a sacrifice fly to
center, scoring Hodges and moving Amoros to third.
Roebuck walked, loading the bases. Neal walked, forcing
in Amoros. Gilliam singled to the pitcher, scoring
Roseboro. Roebuck moved to third and Neal to second.
Bob Kennedy batted for Snider and singled to center, scoring Roebuck and Neal, and moving Gilliam to third.
Phillips then threw a wild pitch, scoring Gilliam and moving Kennedy to second. Cimoli singled to center, scoring
Kennedy. Rookie John DeMerit made a spectacular diving
catch of Hodges' low liner to center to end the inning.
Phillips gave up five hits, walked four men, hit one, made
one wild pitch, and faced thirteen batters as the Dodgers
scored nine runs, to go ahead 20-4, which was the final
score.[13]

Of the twenty runs, Gilliam scored four, Neal and
Amoros three each, Snider and Hodges two each, and one
each by Cimoli, Campanella, Roseboro, Kennedy,
Drysdale, and Roebuck. It was Brooklyn's largest run total
of the season, surpassing their previous high of eleven,
also against Milwaukee.

The Dodgers belted sixteen hits, Gilliam having the
most with four, and collected ten bases on balls One
Milwaukee player who didn't get any hits that night in five
trips to the plate was Aaron, whose fifteen game hitting
streak came to an end. Drysdale earned the victory and
was 7-6. Loser Trowbridge was 3-2.

The Dodgers were now two games out of first place.

Standings	Won	Lost	Pct.	GB
Philadelphia Phillies	48	35	.578	-
St. Louis Cardinals	47	35	.573	½
Milwaukee Braves	47	37	.560	1 ½
Brooklyn Dodgers	45	36	.556	2
Cincinnati Redlegs	46	38	.548	2 ½
New York Giants	39	44	.470	9
Pittsburgh Pirates	30	54	.357	18 ½
Chicago Cubs	27	50	.351	18

Notes to Chapter 2

1. The number two hitter in the National League was Stan Musial of the Cardinals, with a .342 batting average. Among Dodger players, Gino Cimoli was number five, with a .313 average, and Gil Hodges was number seven, with a .308 average.

2. *The New York Times*, July 14, 1957, sec. 5, p. 3.

3. Maglie's nickname came from his reputation for pitching close to batters.

4. Gilliam would go hitless in that day's game, ending his twelve-game hitting streak.

5. Major League Baseball, The Miley Collection, Inc., Brooklyn vs. Milwaukee, July 14, 1957.

6. In *The Artful Dodgers*, Bill Roeder writes: "Gil says he never has become home-run conscious. . . . *Except for occasions when the Dodgers have to go for the long ball to win a game* [italics added], he just tries to meet the ball with an even swing." (Bill Raeder, "(Gil Hodges) The Strong Man" in Tom Meany et. al., *The Artful Dodgers*, p. 84.)

7. *Sports Illustrated*, July 22, 1957, p. 21.

8. *The Wilkes-Barre Record*, July 12, 1957, p. 19.

9. *The Wilkes-Barre Record*, July 15, 1957, p. 12.

10. *Time*, July 22, 1957, p. 62.

11. *Newsweek*, July 22, 1957, p. 78.

12. Mizell's nickname came from his birthplace of Vinegar Bend, Alabama.

13. According to *www.retrosheet.org*, this game ballooned Taylor Phillips' season earned run average from 4.50 to 5.55. In its play-by-play account, *retrosheet* inserted the following wry comment after Gilliam's lead off single in the eighth inning: "Phillips has just entered the twilight zone" (*www.retrosheet.org*).

Chapter 3

"Showing Their Bats"

On Tuesday, July 16, the Pittsburgh Pirates took a pair from the Chicago Cubs in Pittsburgh. The first involved the resumption of a June 16th game between the two teams that had been suspended because of the Pennsylvania Sunday curfew law. It was resumed with the score tied at 4-4 and one man out in the Pirate half of the seventh inning. Chicago pitcher Jim Brosnan got Dee Fondy on an outfield fly before left fielder Frank Thomas hit his thirteenth home run of the season, putting Pittsburgh ahead 5-4. Pitcher Vernon Law garnered his fifth win in nine decisions by setting the Cubs down in order in the two remaining innings of the game. Loser Brosnan was 1-4.

In the regularly scheduled game, Pittsburgh defeated Chicago 5-3. Chicago was ahead 2-0 and pitcher Bob Rush had a one-hit shutout going until the seventh inning when Frank Thomas doubled home two runs then scored on Gene Baker's triple, putting Pittsburgh ahead 3-2. The Pirates added two runs in the eighth on singles by Dee Fondy, shortstop Dick Groat, center fielder Bill Virdon, and Thomas, chasing Rush. The Cubs threatened in the ninth when they got two of their nine hits and scored a run but pitcher Bob Friend survived to complete the game and gain his seventh victory against eleven defeats. Losing pitcher Rush was 1-9.

The New York Giants treated a home crowd to a 6-1 victory over the Cincinnati Redlegs as Willie Mays hit four consecutive singles and second baseman Daryl Spencer drove in four of the Giant runs with a single and two home

runs. Shortstop Eddie Bressoud accounted for the other
two runs with a single and a homer. Winning pitcher
Ruben Gomez struck out four, walked four, and gave up
six hits to earn his eleventh victory against eight defeats.
He also beaned Frank Robinson above the left ear with a
fast ball in the eighth inning, splitting Robinson's protec-
tive helmet and causing the left fielder to crumble at the
plate. Robinson was carried from the field on a stretcher
and first reports said he had suffered a concussion but
there was no sign of a fracture. Hal Jeffcoat, the first of
three Cincinnati pitchers, took the loss and was 8-7.

Warren Spahn pitched a six-hitter and hit a triple to lead
the Milwaukee Braves to a 6-2 win over the Philadelphia
Phillies in Philadelphia. Both Phillie runs were unearned.
The Braves got out in front early when Hank Aaron hit a
two-run homer, his twenty-ninth, in the first inning. Wes
Covington singled home a run in the second, Del Crandall
homered in the fourth, and Spahn's run-scoring triple came
in the sixth. Eddie Mathews doubled home the final run in
the ninth. Philadelphia loaded the bases in their half of the
ninth but right fielder Andy Pafko came through with a
one-handed diving catch of Richie Ashburn's sinking line
drive to end the game. Spahn gained his tenth victory
against seven defeats. Philadelphia starter and loser
Harvey Haddox was 8-6.

The St. Louis Cardinals began a three-game series that
night against the Dodgers in Brooklyn. In the second
inning, Ken Boyer doubled to left against Dodger pitcher
Danny McDevitt. Catcher Hal Smith singled to right, with
Boyer moving to third. Smith then stole second on
McDevitt's pitch from a wind-up. Right fielder Wally
Moon walked, loading the bases. Third baseman Eddie
Kasko singled to left, scoring Boyer and Smith for a 2-0
lead. Carl Erskine relieved McDevitt. St. Louis pitcher

Lindy McDaniel made a sacrifice bunt, advancing Moon to
third base and Kasko to second. Don Blasingame hit a
grounder to third baseman Randy Jackson and Moon got
caught in a rundown between third and home. He was
eventually tagged out by Erskine, with Kasko advancing to
third and Blasingame making it to second. Alvin Dark
tried to push a surprise bunt to the right side for a squeeze
play but he missed Erskine's fast ball. Catcher Roy
Campanella fired a blur to third base to nail Kasko before
he could get back to the bag, ending the inning.

Gino Cimoli opened the Brooklyn fourth with a looping
single to right. Gil Hodges then lashed a drive toward the
scoreboard in right which Wally Moon just missed on a
one-handed stab. Cimoli had rounded third base and
Hodges was headed for that bag when Cimoli held up,
fearing that Moon's throw would get him at the plate.
Moon's toss was wide of the plate, about ten feet up the
third base side. Catcher Smith, expecting a cutoff and
relay by first baseman Stan Musial, covered the plate.
When Musial let the peg go through, it bounced into the
Cardinal dugout and was ruled an automatic two-base
error. Cimoli was waved home. Hodges followed but was
stopped by plate umpire Tony Venzon and sent back to
third. That brought Dodger manager Walter Alston out to
protest and, after a brief conference, Hodges was credited
by the umpires with a double on the hit and was waved
home, tying the score at 2-2. Alston apparently won the
argument by citing the ground rule which says that a runner is entitled to the base he is headed for plus one.
Hodges was headed for third base and was, therefore,
motioned home. That call, in turn, sent Cardinal manager
Fred Hutchinson out to protest and resulted in his being
ejected from the game by third base umpire Shag
Crawford.

A leadoff single to left by Charley Neal in the Dodger

fifth was followed by a hit-and-run double to right-center by Jim Gilliam, scoring Neal. Duke Snider then blasted his twentieth home run of the season, which sailed well over the scoreboard. Cimoli followed with a hit to the right field corner and was cut down trying to stretch it to a double. That was all, however, for McDaniel, who was relieved by Willard Schmidt. Sandy Amoros walked, stole second, and scored on a single through the middle by Campanella, capping a four-run rally that put Brooklyn ahead 6-2.

Reliever Erskine gave up his first run to St. Louis in the seventh inning when Moon singled to right, advanced to second on a grounder by pinch-hitter Dick Schofield, and scored on a double to right by Blasingame.

The Dodgers came back with a run in their half of the seventh on Gil Hodges' homer over the scoreboard, his twelfth of the season, against reliever Hoyt Wilhelm.

In the eighth inning, Cardinal left fielder Del Ennis singled to left and new catcher Hobie Landrith homered but this was the last scoring by St. Louis, giving Brooklyn a 7-5 victory. Winner Erskine was 3-1 and loser McDaniel was 8-6.

Brooklyn announcer Vin Scully exclaimed that the Dodgers were "showing their bats around the league."[1] Wrote Roscoe McGowen: "No other National League team has been able to toss a monkey wrench into the Dodgers' pennant drive since the All-Star game. Last night at Ebbets Field the Brooks won their fifth straight game."[2]

The Dodgers were now one game out of first place.

(Left to right) Al Helfer, Vin Scully, and Jerry Doggett provided radio and television coverage of Dodger games.

Source: 1957 Dodger yearbook.

Standings	Won	Lost	Pct.	GB
Philadelphia Phillies	48	36	.571	-
St. Louis Cardinals	47	36	.566	½
Milwaukee Braves	48	37	.565	½
Brooklyn Dodgers	46	36	.561	1
Cincinnati Redlegs	46	39	.541	2 ½
New York Giants	40	44	.476	8
Pittsburgh Pirates	32	54	.372	1 7
Chicago Cubs	27	52	.342	18 ½

On Wednesday, July 17, George Crowe's bat helped the Cincinnati Redlegs edge the New York Giants 5-4. With

Cincinnati trailing 1-0, the first baseman belted a solo
home run in the second inning, his nineteenth, to tie the
score. He then followed with a three-run homer in the
third to put the Redlegs ahead 4-1, sending Giant starter
Curt Barclay to the showers. What proved to be the winning run for Cincinnati came in the fifth inning when
Johnny Temple doubled off New York reliever Mike
McCormick then went to third on an infield out by Frank
Robinson, who returned to the lineup showing no ill effects
from his beaning of the previous night. Temple then
scored on a wild pitch, for a 5-1 lead. The Giants added a
run in the sixth and another in the eighth at which point
Raul Sanchez relieved Redleg starter Brooks Lawrence.
Sanchez gave up a run in the ninth but held the victory for
Lawrence, who was 10-5. Loser Barclay was 4-7.

The Milwaukee Braves defeated the Philadelphia
Phillies 10-3 in a contest that had a first-inning rhubarb, an
eighteen-minute delay of game, and the ejection of
Philadelphia's starting pitcher Robin Roberts. Roberts
pitched a scoreless top of the first. In the Phillies' half of
the first, there was a disputed double play involving
Granny Hamner and Eddie Bouchee. In the ensuing argument, the usually mild-mannered Roberts was ejected for
calling umpire Jocko Conlon a name and then had to be
restrained by Philadelphia manager Mayo Smith and several of his teammates from attacking Conlon. Beer cans
began to fly from the hometown crowd in the stands and
the ground crew had to clear the field of debris before the
game could be resumed. Philadelphia played the game
under protest. The Braves held a 5-0 lead after five
innings. The Phillies ralled for three runs in the sixth,
knocking out starter Lew Burdette. The Braves then
opened up for five runs in the seventh to seal their victory.
They pounded five Phillie pitchers for thirteen hits, including three by Hank Aaron, who had to leave the game

because of an ankle injury. Milwaukee reliever Don McMahon preserved the win for Burdette, who was 8-6. Losing pitcher Jack Meyer was 0-1.

The Chicago Cubs staged a seventh inning rally to nip the Pittsburgh Pirates 4-3. Pittsburgh was leading 3-2 after six innings when Dale Long pinch-hit for Cub starter Moe Drabowsky and singled. Dave Hillman ran for Long and reached second base on center fielder Bob Will's single. First baseman Bob Speake doubled Hillman home but Will was thrown out at the plate. Speake went to third on the play and scored what proved to be the winning run on a perfect squeeze bunt by Ernie Banks. Drabowsky got his fifth win in thirteen decisions. Loser Ronnie Kline was 2-13.

In game two with the Cardinals, Charley Neal led off the Dodger first inning by beating out a hit to deep short against pitcher Sam Jones. Jim Gilliam lined a single to left, advancing Neal to second. Duke Snider walked on four pitches to load the bases. Gino Cimoli hit into a double play, scoring Neal for a 1-0 lead.

Brooklyn pitcher Don Newcombe retired the first nine men to face him before Don Blasingame led off the St. Louis fourth with a topped roller down the first base line. Newcombe tried twice to pick up the ball and missed both times. It was scored as an infield hit. Alvin Dark followed with a single to left on a hit-and-run play, sending Blasingame to third. Stan Musial sent a long fly to center field which Duke Snider had to leap high against the wall to pull down. Blasingame scored, tying the game at 1-1. Wally Moon then belted his sixteenth home run of the season over the right field screen. Del Ennis doubled into the left field corner and Ken Boyer singled to left, scoring Ennis for a 4-1 Cardinal lead. Ed Roebuck replaced Newcombe and retired the side.

In the top of the fifth, Blasingame beat out a deep bounder to first, with an error on the play by first baseman Gil Hodges. Dark singled to right, sending Blasingame to third. An error by third baseman Randy Jackson allowed Dark to make it to second. Musial was walked intentionally. A wild pitch by Roebuck allowed Blasingame to score, with Dark moving to third and Musial to second. Moon walked, loading the bases. Ennis forced Moon, with Dark scoring the Cardinals' second unearned run, for a 6-1 lead.

In the Dodger half of the sixth, Neal singled to center and Gilliam doubled off the scoreboard, scoring Neal when center fielder Boyer fumbled the ball for an error. The Cardinals' lead was cut to 6-2.

Ennis' thirteenth home run in the eighth inning against Brooklyn's third reliever, Don Bessent, restored a five-run lead for the Redbirds.

Sandy Amoros homered in the ninth for the last Dodger run, giving St. Louis a 7-3 victory. Winner Sam Jones went the distance with a ten-hitter, and had twelve strike-outs and one walk to earn his eighth win against three losses. Loser Don Newcombe was 9-7.[3]

The Dodgers fell back to one-and-a-half games out of first place.

Standings	Won	Lost	Pct.	GB
St. Louis Cardinals	48	36	.571	-
Milwaukee Braves	49	37	.570	-
Philadelphia Phillies	48	37	.565	½
Brooklyn Dodgers	46	37	.554	1 ½
Cincinnati Redlegs	47	39	.547	2
New York Giants	40	45	.471	8 ½
Pittsburgh Pirates	32	55	.364	17 ½
Chicago Cubs	28	52	.350	18

On Thursday, July 18, Philadelphia pitcher Robin Roberts received a telegram from National League President Warren Giles notifying him that he was fined $50.00 and suspended for three days for his part in the ruckus at the previous night's game at Connie Mack Stadium. Giles wrote: "[I] Recognize [the] tension under which you were playing. But any suspension less than this for your actions cannot be justified."[4] Roberts was contrite. "It could have been worse," he said. "If they hadn't stopped me, I could have got into a lot worse trouble."[5]

The Phillies had nothing to cheer about from that day's game either, which they lost to the Milwaukee Braves 4-2. The Braves took a 2-0 lead in the second inning when center fielder John DeMerit, substituting for the ailing Hank Aaron, singled and catcher Del Rice homered. After Philadelphia tied the score in the fifth inning, Milwaukee went ahead 3-2 in the sixth on Frank Torre's triple and Wes Covington's single. In the eighth inning, Torre and Covington were on base when Rice singled Torre home for his third run batted in of the Braves' four runs. The Phillies threatened in the ninth when, with two men out, starter Bob Buhl gave up his second walk of the inning. Reliever Don McMahan struck out Harry Anderson to end the game and give Buhl his tenth victory in sixteen decisions. Losing pitcher Curt Simmons was 9-5.

A four-run rally in the ninth inning enabled the Pittsburgh Pirates to get past the Chicago Cubs 6-5. Trailing 5-2 in the final frame, the Pirates picked up their first run on pinch-hit singles by Roman Mejias and Gene Freese, and a sacrifice fly by Dee Fondy. Bob Skinner walked and Dick Groat tripled to tie the score. With only one out, the Cubs issued two intentional passes, to pinch-hitter Jim Pendleton and Frank Thomas, filling the bases for a possible double play. Second baseman Bill Mazeroski upset this plan with a single that sent Groat

across the plate with the deciding run. Winning pitcher
Luis Arroyo was 3-8. Loser Turk Lown was 4-4.

   Gus Bell's two-run homer in the third inning was all
that the Cincinnati Redlegs needed for a 2-1 victory over
the New York Giants. Winning pitcher Johnny
Klippstein's shutout bid was spoiled in the ninth inning
when Bobby Thomson led off with a home run. After
Eddie Bressoud singled, reliever Raul Sanchez was
brought in. He got pinch-hitter Ossie Virgil to bunt into a
double play and pinch-hitter Hank Sauer to foul out. It
was Klippstein's fourth win against nine defeats. Losing
pitcher Stu Miller suffered his sixth defeat in nine decisions.

Notes to Chapter 3

1. Author recollection.

2. *The New York Times*, July 17, 1957, p. 30.

3. Newcombe's seventh loss equaled his losses for the entire 1956 season, when he compiled an amazing 27-7 record.

4. *The Wilkes-Barre Record*, July 19, 1957, p. 19.

5. Ibid.

Chapter 4

Gil and the Duke

On Saturday, July 13, 1957 my parents, John and Dorothy Nordell, and I left our home in Wilkes-Barre, Pennsylvania for a week's vacation in Silver Beach, New Jersey. We were accompanied by my aunt, Dorothy Nordell, of nearby Kingston, Pennsylvania.

While there we kept track of the National League race by listening to the Brooklyn Dodgers Radio Network and reading the New York *Daily News*. We enjoyed the play-by-play of Dodger announcers Jerry Doggett, Al Helfer, and especially Vin Scully.[1]

We were excited about the Dodgers' growing prospects for winning the pennant but the biggest thrill of all came on July 18 when we left the shore to attend our first game in Brooklyn. Until then we had only viewed Dodger games on our 1953 black and white RCA television set.

My first sight of Ebbets Field in real life color was breathtaking – the bright green grass, the stands, the right field wall and screen, the Schaefer Beer scoreboard, and, above all, the players. We had box seats along the left field line, shortly beyond third base. Emmett Kelly, a for-mer circus clown who entertained the fans in 1957 as the renowned Brooklyn Bum, walked by our area prior to game time and posed for a picture for my father.[2]

The starting pitchers were Johnny Podres, 7-3, for the Dodgers and Larry Jackson, 10-5, for the Cardinals. The game began at 1:30 P.M.

In the bottom of the first inning, with one out, Jim Gilliam walked then stole second base, his hat flying off as

Emmett Kelly, a former clown with the Ringling Brothers and Barnum and Bailey Circus, appears as the renowned Brooklyn Bum before game time.

Source: John R. Nordell.

he came in underneath catcher Hal Smith's wide throw to shortstop Alvin Dark. Duke Snider also walked then Gino Cimoli flied out to center field and Gil Hodges flied out to left, to end the inning.

In the third inning, Snider put the Dodgers on the scoreboard with a home run, his twenty-first, deep into the lower center field seats, just above the 393-foot marker.

Stan "The Man" Musial began the fourth inning for the Cardinals with a double to right, the six-hundredth double of his major league career, then scored on a single to center by Del Ennis, tying the game 1-1.

In the fifth inning, Podres singled to right, Charley Neal walked, and Gilliam doubled to right, scoring both runners and putting the Dodgers ahead 3-1.

In the eighth inning, Eddie Miksis pinch-hit for Jackson and singled to left. Dark doubled to left, scoring Miksis for the Cardinals' second run.

In the bottom of the eighth, Snider singled to center off new St. Louis pitcher Willard Schmidt, moved to second when Sandy Amoros was walked intentionally, then scored on Roy Campanella's single to left, making the score 4-2 for Brooklyn.

Ken Boyer opened the top of the ninth inning with a single to left, whereupon Dodger manager Walter Alston replaced Podres with Clem Labine. Joe Cunningham, pinch-hitting for Smith, singled to right. Wally Moon struck out. Eddie Kasko doubled into the left field corner, scoring Boyer and Cunningham and tying the game 4-4. Hobie Landrith, pinch-hitting for Schmidt, singled to center, scoring Kasko and chasing Labine. Don Blasingame hit a grounder off new pitcher Danny McDevitt. First baseman Gil Hodges fielded the ball then dropped it as he was about to throw to second for a force play. Dark was called out on strikes. Musial singled through a hole left by Neal at short when McDevitt missed a pick-off sign, scor-

Cardinal ace Larry Jackson versus Dodger slugger Duke Snider. Third base coach Billy Herman looks on.

Source: John R. Nordell.

ing Landrith. Del Ennis tripled off the center field wall, scoring Blasingame and Musial. Boyer walked, with St. Louis having batted around the lineup. Cunningham singled to center, scoring Ennis. McDevitt threw a wild pitch and Cunningham took second base. Moon grounded to first for the third out. Twelve Cardinals had come to the plate and seven had scored.

Now trailing 9-4, the Dodgers came to bat in the bottom of the ninth. Carl Furillo, pinch-hitting for McDevitt, beat out a dribbler down the third base line against new Cardinal pitcher Hoyt Wilhelm. Neal and Gilliam walked. With the bases loaded, Brooklyn fans stirred with anticipation as Snider came to bat. Cardinal manager Fred Hutchinson replaced Wilhelm with lefthander "Vingar Bend" Mizell. Snider grounded out to first, scoring Furillo. By now, Mizell's pitching motion had drawn the attention of the fans. They whooped in a rhythmic chant as he leaned way back, nearly touching the mound with the ball, before springing forward to release the pitch. Cimoli walked, again loading the bases and bringing Hodges to the plate. There were more elongated pitches from Mizell and more chants from the crowd. Then, with the count at one ball and one strike, there was a mighty blow from Hodges. As the ball sailed into the lower left-center field seats, it seemed as if all of the 22,059 fans in Ebbets Field jumped to their feet in a full-throated roar. It was Hodges' thirteenth home run of the season and the twelfth grand slam of his career, tying the National League record for grand slams held by Rogers Hornsby and Ralph Kiner. The score was tied 9-9. Mizell walked Amoros and was replaced by Herm Wehmeier but not before receiving a tirade from manager Hutchinson. Amoros stole second. Campanella grounded out to the pitcher, who held Amoros to the bag. Pee Wee Reese, who had replaced Randy Jackson at third base in the eighth, hit a looping fly out to second, sending the contest into extra innings.

In the tenth, Roger Craig, the new Brooklyn reliever, walked the first two batters to face him, Kasko and Landrith. Blasingame fouled out to the catcher and Dick Schofield, who replaced Dark at shortstop in the ninth, was called out on strikes. Walker Cooper, pinch-hitting for Wehmeier, flew out to left field, to end the inning.

In the bottom of the tenth, Craig grounded to third against new St. Louis reliever Lloyd Merritt. Neal struck out and Gilliam popped out to third.

In the eleventh inning, Ennis was called out on strikes, Boyer struck out, and Cunningham popped out to first.

In the home half of the eleventh, Snider lined a double off the right-center field wall. Cimoli bunted and Snider dashed for third. Merritt fielded the ball just to his right and saw a chance to nail Snider. As Snider slid into the bag, Merritt's throw got away from Kasko for an error and, amidst cheers from the fans and his teammates, the Duke

Gil Hodges (14) and teammates Gino Cimoli (crossing the plate), Charley Neal (43), Jim Gilliam (19), and Sandy Amoros (15) after Hodges' grand slam. Catcher Hobie Landrith (16) and umpire Bill Jackowski watch.

Source: 1958 Dodger yearbook.

raced home with the winning run, 10-9. Craig earned the victory and was 5-5. Merritt took the loss and was 1-2.

The Dodgers remained one-and-a-half games out of first place but moved from fourth place to third.

Standings	Won	Lost	Pct.	GB
Milwaukee Braves	50	37	.575	-
St. Louis Cardinals	48	37	.565	1
Brooklyn Dodgers	47	37	.560	1 ½
Philadelphia Phillies	48	38	.558	1 ½
Cincinnati Redlegs	48	39	.552	2
New York Giants	40	46	.465	9 ½
Pittsburgh Pirates	33	55	.375	17 ½
Chicago Cubs	28	53	.346	19

On Friday, July 19, the Cincinnati Redlegs defeated the Philadelphia Phillies 7-2 at Connie Mack Stadium on the strength of fourteen singles and one home run. The homer, a two-run smash by George Crowe, his twenty-first, came in the third inning off pitcher Jack Sanford and gave the Redlegs a 2-1 lead. A five-run rally in the fifth inning knocked out Sanford, who exited after allowing a run to score with a wild pitch. Don Hoak was in the lineup for Cincinnati for the first time since July 11. He contributed a single to the rally and scored a run, going one-for-five. Winner Joe Nuxhall went the distance and was 4-5. Losing pitcher Sanford was 12-3.

Thirty-six-year-old Andy Pafko, the oldest player on the Milwaukee Braves, starred at bat and in the outfield as he led his team to a 3-1 victory over the New York Giants at the Polo Grounds. Shifted to the cleanup spot in the batting order, with Hank Aaron still out with a sprained ankle, Pafko belted the first of his two home runs in the second inning off pitcher Johnny Antonelli to give the Braves a

(Top to bottom) Duke Snider slides into third base as Eddie Kasko bobbles the throw and umpire Lee Ballanfant watches.

Source: *Daily News* (**New York**).

(Top) As Eddie Kasko chases the ball, Duke Snider
heads for home and (bottom) is greeted by manager
Walter Alston (24) and teammates Don Zimmer (23),
Elmer Valo (3), and Sandy Koafax (32).

Source: *Daily News* (New York).

1-0 lead. New York tied the game in the fourth inning and it remained a pitchers' duel between Gene Conley and Antonelli until the ninth when Pafko's two-run homer proved decisive. In the second inning, right fielder Pafko had to go far back to haul in a Bobby Thomson fly ball and in the eighth, with a man on first, he made a diving catch of a sinking liner by pinch-hitter Dusty Rhodes. Milwaukee's Red Schoendienst hit safely in his sixteenth straight game. Winner Conley gained his third victory against four defeats. Loser Antonelli was 9-8.

Vernon Law pitched shutout ball as the Pittsburgh Pirates blanked the St. Louis Cardinals 7-0 at Forbes Field. Bill Virdon led the assault on the Cardinals with a single, double, and triple in four trips to the plate. The triple came in the first inning and was followed by Frank Thomas' fourteenth home run as the Pirates jumped to a 2-0 lead. Nine of Pittsburgh's twelve hits came at the expense of starting pitcher Von McDaniel, who left in the sixth inning. The Cardinals got nine singles but stranded them all and none reached third base. Winner Law gained his sixth victory in ten decisions. Losing pitcher McDaniel was 4-2.

The Chicago Cubs met the Dodgers for a twilight-night doubleheader at Ebbets Field. Also scheduled was the long-planned "Gil Hodges Night."

In the first inning of the opener, Charley Neal hit a bloop single to right field off Chicago pitcher Don Elston. Neal was picked off first base but made it safely to second on an error by Elston. Sandy Amoros singled to center, scoring Neal and giving Brooklyn a 1-0 lead.

In the third inning, Chicago second baseman Bobby Morgan hit a home run off Dodger pitcher Sandy Koafax to tie the game.

In the seventh inning, left fielder Lee Walls homered to put the Cubs ahead 2-1. The two home runs were the only hits that Koafax gave up in seven innings and he struck out eleven. He was lifted for a pinch-hitter in the Dodger seventh and reliever Don Bessent took the mound in the eighth inning.

In the Dodger half of the eighth, Jim Gilliam walked and Duke Snider singled to short, with Gilliam making it to second. Amoros singled to right, scoring Gilliam and tying the game 2-2. With no scoring in the ninth, the game went into extra innings.

In the tenth inning, Walls hit the first pitch by new Dodger reliever Clem Labine for his second home run of the game, putting Chicago ahead 3-2.

With one out in the home half of the tenth, Snider belted a home run, his twenty-second, deep into the left-center field seats to again tie the game. Gil Hodges got an infield hit to third, which was his only hit of the game. Elston was relieved by Dick Littlefield, who walked Amoros on four pitches. Littlefield, in turn, gave way to reliever Turk Lown who got Gino Cimoli to hit into a force out on Amoros. Hodges advanced to third. Then catcher Johnny Roseboro, who had replaced Roy Campanella in the seventh, knocked a three-run homer over the scoreboard – his first home run and only his third hit in the major leagues – giving the Dodgers a 6-3 victory. Labine earned the win and was 4-5. Elston took the loss and was 2-3.

Between the games, Gil Hodges had his "night" as he was showered with gifts, including a sleek white Dodge convertible and a silver serving tray from his Dodger teammates that was engraved with their autographs. He got a couple of kisses from Joann Duffy, the president of the Gil Hodges Fan Club. He also received numerous tributes from personal friends and notables, among them a telegram of congratulations from President Eisenhower. With Hodges that evening were his wife Joan and their three children. His parents, brother, and sister flew in from

Indiana for the occasion. After forty-five minutes of cere-
monies, Hodges addressed his fans:

> Thank you very much. I'd like to take
> this opportunity to thank Joann Duffy
> and Al Bonnie [chairman of the Hodges
> Committee]. To all you friends, all I
> can say is I thank you from the bottom
> of my heart for making this wonderful
> evening for me and my family. May
> God bless you.[3]

Hodges' dad, Charles, threw out the first ball to start the
second game. It was a strike to his son.

In the first inning, Jim Gilliam beat out a bunt toward
third base against Cub pitcher Tom Poholsky and moved to
second when Duke Snider walked. Gil Hodges then hit a
line single to left that scored Gilliam for a 1-0 lead and
produced the 1,000th run-batted-in of his career. When
that fact was announced to the 28,724 fans, the cheering
was even louder than during the earlier festivities.

In the third inning, Snider swatted his second home run
of the night and his seventh in nine games. This one landed on Snider's usual target, Bedford Avenue, and put the
Dodgers ahead 2-0.

Chicago's Ernie Banks ended pitcher Sal Maglie's no-
hitter in the fourth inning with his eighteenth home run of
the year, cutting the Dodgers' lead to one run.

In the bottom of the fourth, Johnny Roseboro, who
caught the second game, walked then was forced at second
by Pee Wee Reese. Maglie hit a sacrifice bunt that
advanced Reese to second. Neal singled to left, scoring
Reese and giving Brooklyn a 3-1 lead.

In the sixth inning, Chicago's Bob Speake homered and

(Top) Johnny Roseboro is congratulated by Randy Jackson (2),
Gino Cimoli (9), Gil Hodges, and batboy Eddie Lehan while
umpire Frank Dascoli watches. (Bottom) Gil Hodges and his
family sit in a Dodge convertible on "Gil Hodges Night."

Sources: (Top) 1958 Dodger yearbook; (bottom) *1958 Who's
Who in Sports.*

a pair of doubles by Walt Moryn and pinch-hitter Chuck
Tanner tied the game 3-3.

In the Dodger half of the sixth, Roseboro hit a double
near the left field line. Reese walked then Randy Jackson,
pinch-hitting for Maglie, lined a single to center, scoring
Roseboro. Gilliam doubled to the right field corner, scoring Reese for what proved to be a decisive 5-3 lead.

Reliever Ed Roebuck took over in the seventh inning,
allowing only one hit and holding the Cubs scoreless for
the rest of the game, preserving Maglie's fourth win in six
decisions. Loser Poholsky was 1-5.

With their first doubleheader triumph of the year, the
Dodgers were now one game out of first place and moved
from third place to second.

Standings	Won	Lost	Pct.	GB
Milwaukee Braves	51	37	.580	-
Brooklyn Dodgers	49	37	.570	1
St. Louis Cardinals	48	38	.558	2
Cincinnati Redlegs	49	39	.557	2
Philadelphia Phillies	48	39	.552	2 ½
New York Giants	40	47	.460	10 ½
Pittsburgh Pirates	34	55	.382	17 ½
Chicago Cubs	28	55	.337	20 ½

Notes to Chapter 4

1. One of the commercial sponsors of the games, the
F. & M. Schaefer Brewing Company of Brooklyn, had a
catchy jingle:

> "For real, real enjoyment, get Schaefer,
> Schaefer beer.
>> For real, real enjoyment,
>> get *S c h a e f e r.*
>> It's *r e a l* beer.
> For real, real refreshment, ask for Schaefer,
> Schaefer beer.
>> For real, real refreshment,
>> ask for *S c h a e f e r.*
>> It's *r e a l* beer."

(Major League Baseball, The Miley Collection, Inc.,
Brooklyn vs. Milwaukee, July 14, 1957.)

2. Kelly had starred with the Ringling Brothers and
Barnum and Bailey Circus and was, says Damon Rice,
"the most famous clown in America" (Damon Rice,
Seasons Past, p. 426).

3. *The Sporting News,* July 31, 1957, p. 23. Roscoe
McGowen would write what Dodger fans everywhere
must have felt: "Gil Hodges couldn't have picked a better time for his twelfth grand-slam than the day before
his 'night'." (Ibid., p. 15.)

Chapter 5

High Tide

On Saturday, July 20, Del Ennis drove in four runs and
Eddie Kasko accounted for two more as the St. Louis
Cardinals put together an eighteen-hit attack to down the
Pittsburgh Pirates 9-4. Both teams scored two runs in the
first inning but the Cardinals took a four-run lead in the
third when Ennis hit a three-run homer, his fourteenth, then
Ken Boyer singled, stole second, and scored on a single by
Kasko, knocking out Pittsburgh starter Bob Friend. A
double by Boyer and a single by Kasko added another run
in the fifth. The Cardinals scored their last two runs in the
eighth when reliever Lloyd Merritt walked then Don
Blasingame and Alvin Dark doubled. Starter Murrey
Dickson, who pitched seven innings, got credit for the victory and was 5-2. Friend was tagged with his twelfth
defeat in nineteen decisions.

The Philadelphia Phillies defeated the Cincinnati
Redlegs 7-5 in a come-from-behind, ninth inning victory.
The Phillies scored runs in the first and second innings and
Harry Anderson hit a two-run homer in the third, routing
Cincinnati starter Hal Jeffcoat. The Redlegs, in turn,
chased Philadelphia starter Jim Hearn with a three-run
rally in the fourth and scored two more in the fifth off
reliever Warren Hacker. The Phillies came to bat in the
bottom of the ninth, trailing 5-4. With one out, pinch-hitter
Chuck Harmon beat out an infield single and Richie
Ashburn walked against reliever Don Gross. Stan Lopata
pinch-hit for second baseman Solly Hemus and hit a game-

ending homer. The victory went to reliever Dick Farrell who was 4-2. Loser Gross was 4-6.

The Milwaukee Braves broke a late innings tie to defeat the New York Giants 7-5. The Braves jumped to a 3-0 lead in the second inning when Johnny Logan tripled, John DeMerit singled, Red Schoendienst doubled, extending his hitting streak to seventeen games, and Frank Torre singled, sending Giant starter Ruben Gomez to the showers. Home runs by Del Crandall in the third and Wes Covington in the seventh made it 5-0. Bob Trowbridge pitched three-hit, shutout ball through seven innings and had two outs in the eighth when an outfield error by Crandall sparked a five-run rally by the Giants, chasing Trowbridge and reliever Don McMahon. Second reliever Ernie Johnson finally got the third out. In the Milwaukee ninth, Eddie Mathews singled and Covington hit his second homer of the game off New York's fourth pitcher, Marv Grissom. Johnson put the Giants down in order in the ninth for the win and was 5-1. Loser Grissom was 2-3.[1]

The Dodgers and the Cubs met for a third game at Ebbets Field on July 20. In the first inning, Bob Speake singled to center field off pitcher Don Drysdale, advanced to third on a double to left-center by Ernie Banks, and scored when Walt Moryn grounded out to first.

With two men out in the bottom of the first, Duke Snider walked then Gil Hodges lined a sizzler straight at the mound. The ball caromed off the right hand of pitcher Dave Hillman and went for a hit, with Snider moving to second. Hillman suffered a split nail on the middle finger and had to leave the game. Sandy Amoros hit a double off the right field screen against reliever Don Kaiser, scoring Snider. Gino Cimoli also doubled off the right field screen, scoring Hodges and Amoros, and made it to third on an error by center fielder Bob Will. Randy Jackson singled to left-center, scoring Cimoli for a 4-1 Brooklyn lead.

In the sixth inning, Jackson fattened the Dodgers' lead to 5-1 with a home run to the center field seats, his first homer of the season, off Cub reliever Jim Brosnan.

Pinch-hitter Chuck Tanner led off the seventh inning for Chicago with a single to right which was followed by a walk to another pinch-hitter, Dale Long. Will hit into a third-to-first double play, with Long moving to second. Speake got on first when second baseman Jim Gilliam bobbled a grounder, with Long advancing to third. Banks then connected for a home run, his nineteenth, cutting Brooklyn's lead to 5-4. When Moryn singled to right, manager Walter Alston relieved Drysdale with Clem Labine, who ended the inning.

Dodger announcer Jerry Doggett referred to "the crazy, mixed up National League standings" and noted that the Dodgers would take over first place if they defeated the Cubs and the Braves lost their game against the Giants.[2] Brooklyn fans were aware of this and cheered loudly in the bottom of the seventh when the scoreboard showed the Giants coming back from a 5-0 deficit to tie the Braves at 5-5.

Duke Snider led off the bottom of the eighth against third Cub reliever Dick Drott by giving the Dodgers an insurance run and himself a milestone with a mighty blast over the right field screen that bounced from Bedford Avenue atop a garage and then into a parking lot. It was the Duke's twenty-fourth home run, his eighth in ten games, and the 300th of his career. He was tied with Chuck Klein for thirteenth on the all-time home run list and only needed two more homers to pass Rogers Hornsby. Hodges walked then advanced to second on a grounder by Amoros. After Cimoli walked, Jackson hit a line single to left, scoring Hodges. It was Jackson's third run batted in of the game, giving Brooklyn a 7-4 lead, and chasing Drott. Reliever Turk Lown ended the inning.

Banks hit his second homer of the game in the ninth but it was the last run for the Cubs, giving Brooklyn a 7-5 victory. Labine earned his eleventh save in relief. Drysdale gained his eighth win against six losses and was tied with teammate Johnny Podres for the best earned run average, 3.00, among National League hurlers.[3] Loser Hillman was 1-7.

The Dodgers remained one game out of first place.

Standings	Won	Lost	Pct.	GB
Milwaukee Braves	52	37	.584	-
Brooklyn Dodgers	50	37	.575	1
St. Louis Cardinals	49	38	.563	2
Philadelphia Phillies	49	39	.557	2 ½
Cincinnati Redlegs	49	40	.551	3
New York Giants	40	48	.455	11 ½
Pittsburgh Pirates	34	56	.378	18 ½
Chicago Cubs	28	56	.333	21 ½

On Sunday, July 21, all of the National League teams played doubleheaders.

The New York Giants came from behind to win the opening game against the Milwaukee Braves 5-4. The Giants scored two runs off starter Warren Spahn in the fourth inning when a double by Willie Mays was followed by Bobby Thomson's eleventh home run of the season. All of Milwaukee's runs came in the eighth inning on three singles, a walk, and two New York errors, chasing starter Ray Crone. The walk was given to Hank Aaron, pinch-hitting for Spahn, who played in his first game since his July 17th injury. Giant Eddie Bressoud homered off reliever Dave Jolly in the bottom of the eighth to narrow the

(Top left) Carl Furillo had a dangerous bat and was an expert at fielding hits off Ebbets Field's right field wall and screen.

(Top right) Clem Labine was the workhorse of the Brooklyn bullpen. He had fine control, a great curve, and a sinker.

(Bottom left) Team captain Pee Wee Reese was the longest serving member of the Dodgers. He shared third base duties.

(Bottom right) Don Drysdale had a live fast ball, a wicked side-arm motion, and lots of strikeouts. He could hit too.

Sources: (Top and bottom left) Dodger photos; (bottom right) News Colorfotos.

Braves' lead to 4-3. Bressoud also began the winning rally in the bottom of the ninth. With two out, he singled off reliever Don McMahon and pinch-hitter Ray Jablonski followed with a twisting fly to short left that fell in for a hit. On the throw to the plate, Bressoud went to third and Jablonski to second. Both runners then scored on pinch-hitter Hank Sauer's game-winning single to left. New York's fourth pitcher, Stu Miller, earned the victory and was 4-6. Losing pitcher McMahon was 0-1.

In the second game, Milwaukee overcame a 4-0 deficit to win 7-4. The Giants scored two runs in both the second and fourth innings off starter Lew Burdette. Johnny Logan, who was five for five, opened the seventh inning for the Braves with a home run. Singles by John DeMerit and Red Schoendienst and a triple by Frank Torre narrowed the Giants' lead to 4-3 and chased starter Curt Barclay. A two-run homer by Del Crandall off reliever Johnny Antonelli in the eighth put Milwaukee ahead 5-4 and four singles by the Braves in the ninth produced two more runs. Schoendienst's two hits in the first game and three hits in the second extended his hitting streak to nineteen games. Reliever Ernie Johnson got the win and was 6-1. Loser Antonelli was 9-9.

The St. Louis Cardinals defeated the Pittsburgh Pirates 7-3 in the opener. St. Louis was outhit 11-7 by Pittsburgh but two hits by Don Blasingame produced four of the Cardinals' runs. Blasingame hit a two-run homer in the third inning and the Cardinals added a run in the fourth on Stan Musial's walk, Wally Moon's double, and Del Ennis' sacrifice fly. The Pirates scored two runs in the sixth inning and one in the eighth to tie the game 3-3 and send it into extra innings. A two-run single by Blasingame sparked a four-run rally by St. Louis in the tenth inning for the victory. Willard Schmidt, the third of four Cardinal pitchers, got the win and was 8-1. The second of three Pirate pitchers, Luis Arroyo, took the loss and was 3-9.

St. Louis pitcher Lindy McDaniel got off to a shaky start in the nightcap, allowing two Pittsburgh runs in the first inning. He went on to become the star of the game, blanking the Pirates thereafter and swatting four hits in five trips to the plates. Eddie Kasko and Ken Boyer also collected four hits as the Cardinals scored four runs in the second inning, two in the third, three in the sixth, and two in the eighth for an 11-2 lead. Pirate starter Bob Purkey was lifted in the second inning after allowing seven hits. With one out in the St. Louis half of the ninth, the umpires called the contest at 7:00 P.M. because of Pennsylvania's Sunday curfew law. A resumed game was scheduled for later in the season.[4]

The Cincinnati Redlegs downed the Philadelphia Phillies 4-2 in the opener as Robin Roberts suffered his seventh successive defeat and served up two home run pitches to add to his unhappy total of twenty-eight for the season. Cincinnati pitcher Brooks Lawrence doubled in a run in the third inning, George Crowe connected for a two-run homer in the fourth, and Gus Bell hit a solo home run in the seventh. Lawrence needed help from relievers Raul Sanchez and Hershell Freeman in earning his eleventh victory against five defeats. Loser Roberts was 6-13.

Ted Kluszewski, Roy McMillan, and right fielder Wally Post collected three hits each, and Gus Bell hit his second home run of the day, an inside-the-parker, as Cincinnati clinched the second game 6-4 in an eleven-hit attack. Redleg starter Art Fowler pitched shutout ball for five innings but was chased by a three-run Philadelphia rally in the sixth. Reliever Tom Acker ended the scoring but, in turn, needed help from reliever Johnny Klippstein when the Phillies rallied for another run in the ninth. Winning pitcher Fowler was 1-0. Loser Harvey Haddox was 8-7.

The Dodgers and the Cubs wrapped up their five-game series that day, which also concluded the Dodgers' post-All-Star game home stand at Ebbets Field.

Charley Neal opened the first inning for Brooklyn with a home run, his seventh, over the right-center field screen off pitcher Moe Drabowsky.

In the third inning, third baseman Bobby Adams doubled to center and Walt Moryn hit his thirteenth home run off Dodger pitcher Carl Erskine, for a 2-1 Chicago lead.

Fifth inning homers by Chuck Tanner and Lee Walls increased the Cubs' lead to 4-1.

In the home half of the fifth, Carl Furillo pinch-hit for Erskine and got a base on balls. Neal singled to left and Duke Snider walked, filling the bases. Gil Hodges singled to left, scoring Furillo and Neal, and narrowing Chicago's lead to 4-3.

Bobby Morgan doubled off reliever Roger Craig in the sixth and came home on a single by Ernie Banks, giving Chicago an insurance run.

In the bottom of the sixth, Gino Cimoli hit an infield single to the pitcher, Randy Jackson singled to left, and Neal singled to left, scoring Cimoli and again cutting the Cubs' lead to one run.

In the Dodger seventh, Hodges singled to left and Sandy Amoros walked. Cimoli lined a sharp single to right and third base coach Billy Herman waived Hodges home. Right fielder Moryn's strike throw to catcher Cal Neeman caught Hodges, who represented the tying run, by a good six feet. Drabowsky was replaced by Turk Lown, who ended the inning.

In the the Dodgers' last at bat, Snider walked. Johnny Roseboro ran for him and moved to second on a sacrifice bunt by Hodges. Lown was replaced by Dick Littlefield

who got Amoros to fly out to short right field. Don Elston
was then brought in to pitch to Cimoli. After going to a
full count, Cimoli fouled to third baseman Adams for the
final out of the game and a 5-4 Chicago victory.
Brooklyn's latest winning streak was ended at four games.
Winner Drabowsky, who celebrated his twenty-second
birthday, was 6-8. Loser Erskine was 3-2.

In the third inning under the lights, Bobby Morgan
walked and Bob Speake hit a home run off Dodger pitcher
Don Newcombe to give the Cubs a 2-0 lead. It was
Newcombe's twenty-second gopher pitch of the year. The
righthander had to leave the game after four innings. He
had inflamed an injury on the middle finger of his pitching
hand when he fouled off a pitch while at bat in the second
inning. Clem Labine took over in relief.

In the bottom of the fourth, Gino Cimoli singled to center off Cub pitcher Bob Rush. Catcher Rube Walker drew
a pass and and right fielder Carl Furillo singled to center,
loading the bases. Duke Snider pinch-hit for Newcombe,
having missed the starting lineup of the second game due
to aggravating an old left knee injury. The Duke singled to
center, scoring Cimoli and Walker, and tying the game.
Rush walked Charley Neal to again load the bases. When
he walked Jim Gilliam, which brought home another run,
he was replaced by Jim Brosnan. Sandy Amoros hit an
infield single to first, scoring Snider. Gil Hodges hit a sacrifice fly to left, scoring Neal, and giving Brooklyn a 5-2
lead.

In the fifth inning, Furillo doubled to left off new
Chicago reliever Tom Poholsky. Labine singled to left,
which was only his second hit of the year, scoring Furillo
for a 6-2 lead.

In the sixth inning, Hodges hit a triple high off the left
field wall and scored on Randy Jackson's sacrifice fly to

center field, giving the Dodgers their 7-2 victory margin. Winner Labine was 5-5. Loser Rush was 1-10.

The Dodgers remained in second place, one game out of first.

Standings	Won	Lost	Pct.	GB
Milwaukee Braves	53	38	.589	-
Brooklyn Dodgers	51	38	.573	1
St. Louis Cardinals	50	38	.568	1 ½
Cincinnati Redlegs	51	40	.560	2
Philadelphia Phillies	49	41	.544	3 ½
New York Giants	41	49	.456	11 ½
Pittsburgh Pirates	34	57	.374	19
Chicago Cubs	29	57	.337	21 ½

No games were scheduled for the National League on Monday, July 22. Early the next morning the Dodgers flew out of LaGuardia Airport in their brand-new, forty-four passenger Convair and headed for St. Louis.

The "Baseball X-Ray" section of the new issue of *Sports Illustrated* included pictures of Duke Snider and Gil Hodges at the top of the page. The caption read:

> **THE BROOKLYN DODGERS** have won nine out of 11 since the All- Star Game. Largely responsible for this surge are Duke Snider, who during this period hit eight home runs, including the 300th of his career, and Gil Hodges, who just tied Rogers Hornsby's N.L. lifetime record of 12 grand slammers and drove in his 1,000th run.[5]

Duke Snider and Gil Hodges, as featured in *Sports Illustrated.*

On Tuesday, July 23, the Pittsburgh Pirates outlasted the
Cincinnati Redlegs to win a fifteen inning marathon 6-3 at
Crosley Field in Cincinnati. Pittsburgh's Bob Skinner connected for a two-run homer in the fifth inning off pitcher
Johnny Klippstein. Cincinnati scored a run in the fifth
inning and again in the ninth to tie the score at 2-2 and
send the game into extra innings. Skinner blasted his second homer in the twelfth off reliever Brooks Lawrence but
the Redlegs tied it at 3-3 in the home half. Skinner's opening single off Lawrence in the fifteenth inning sparked a
decisive three-run rally by the Pirates involving an infield
error by Lawrence on a bunt by Bill Virdon, singles by
Dick Groat and Frank Thomas, and a double by Bill
Mazeroski. Vernon Law, who scattered nine hits and was
on the mound through all but the last two outs of the game,
won his seventh game in eleven decisions. Loser
Lawrence was 11-6.

Bob Buhl pitched a two-hit shutout to give the Milwaukee Braves a 1-0 victory over the Philadelphia Phillies at County Stadium in Milwaukee. Buhl allowed only one batter to get as far as second base. The Braves' lone run came in the second inning when Del Crandall singled and Johnny Logan got his seventh straight hit with a triple off pitcher Curt Simmons. Logan's string ended when he grounded out in the seventh inning. Red Schoendienst singled for Milwaukee in the eighth to extend his hitting streak to twenty games. Winner Buhl was 11-6. Losing pitcher Simmons, who pitched a six-hitter and went the distance for Philadelphia, was 9-6.

Dick Drott pitched a four-hit shutout as the Chicago Cubs defeated the New York Giants 4-0 at Wrigley Field in Chicago. Drott walked only one batter and struck out fourteen with his overpowering speed and curve. It was Drott's third shutout and his total of 112 strikouts for the season boosted him to second place among National League hurlers, behind Philadelphia's Jack Sanford with 116. The Cubs took a 3-0 lead in the fourth inning on singles by Bob Speake and Ernie Banks, a double by Walt Moryn, and an error following an infield hit by Lee Walls, sending Giant pitcher Ramon Monzant to the showers. Speake added a fourth run with a homer off reliever Stu Miller in the fifth inning. Winner Drott was 9-8. Venezuelan Monzant took the loss and was 0-1.

Only five days after their last game at Ebbets Field, the Dodgers and the Cardinals met again at Busch Stadium in St. Louis on the night of July 23. The Dodgers had the same starter, Johnny Podres. On the mound for the Cardinals was Sam Jones, who had ended Brooklyn's five-game winning streak on July 17.

Gil Hodges opened the top of the second inning with a single to left and he reached second when left fielder Del

Pitcher Johnny Podres holds five baseballs to indicate the number of times he had shut out opposing teams in 1957.

Source: Associated Press.

Ennis fumbled the ball. Sandy Amoros and Gino Cimoli walked, to load the bases, then Rube Walker lined Jones' first pitch to right field for a single, scoring Hodges.

Jones retired the next fifteen Dodgers to face him, from the second to the seventh innings, before leaving for a pinch-hitter in the eighth. He didn't receive any help at bat from his teammates, however, and one run was all that Brooklyn needed for a 1-0 victory.

Podres put down St. Louis threats in the first and sixth innings and, in between, retired fourteen straight batters in pitching a five-hitter for his eighth win in eleven decisions.

It was Podres' fifth shutout of the season, in which he led the major leagues. Losing pitcher Jones was 8-4.[6]

The Dodgers remained one game out of first place. It was as close as they would come to capturing the top spot during the remainder of the season.

Standings	Won	Lost	Pct.	GB
Milwaukee Braves	54	38	.587	-
Brooklyn Dodgers	52	38	.578	1
St. Louis Cardinals	50	39	.562	2 ½
Cincinnati Redlegs	51	41	.554	3
Philadelphia Phillies	49	42	.538	4 ½
New York Giants	41	50	.451	12 ½
Pittsburgh Pirates	35	57	.380	19
Chicago Cubs	30	57	.345	21 ½

Notes to Chapter 5

1. Milwaukee's eighth inning outfield error resulted from it being one of the most injury-plagued teams in baseball. The error occurred when Del Crandall dropped a fly ball that appeared to reporter Louis Effrat to be "an easy catch" (*The New York Times,* July 21, 1957, sec. 5, p. 2). Crandall, a catcher, was playing right field because Andy Pafko, the hero of the previous day's game, was sidelined with an injured back. With Bill Bruton and Hank Aaron still on the injured list, the Braves had a serious shortage of outfielders, causing Crandall to be drafted for an unfamiliar position. Shortstop Felix Mantilla was still out because of his July 11th collision with Bruton and first baseman Joe Adcock was also benched from injuries.

2. Major League Baseball, The Miley Collection, Inc., Brooklyn vs. Chicago, July 20, 1957.

3. Vin Scully had a couple of anecdotes about Don Drysdale that day. Noting that the pitcher would celebrate his twenty-first birthday on July 23, Scully went on to say:

> And boy, you should see some of the birthday cards that young Don received from the fair sex. . . . And oh, he's gettin' those mushy cards with the violets and the little hearts on them. And getting quite a ribbing about it too. (Ibid.)

When Drysdale came to bat for the first time that day, Scully reminded listeners that Drysdale had hit two home runs that year and added that a letter received from the father of a young fan had been passed on to Drysdale. Remarked Scully:

> The father wrote us a note and said
> that he had taken his young boy to three
> major league ball games. In each of the
> three games, Drysdale was the starting
> pitcher and in each game Drysdale hit a
> home run. So, as the father finished off
> the letter, he said you can have your
> [Willie] Mays's and [Mickey] Mantles
> and [Duke] Sniders and [Ted] Williams's.
> As far as my boy is concerned, the home
> run king is Don Drysdale. (Ibid.)

4. The suspension of the second game kept intact the National League consecutive playing record of Stan Musial. The Cardinals' thirty-six-year-old star had announced after the All-Star game that he was going to sit out the second game of doubleheaders. Musial ran his streak to 862 games in the opener but sat out the second game. With the suspension, however, Musial still had a chance to extend his record-breaking string by appearing in the resumed game. He did so on August 27 by entering the game as a runner for Ken Boyer, then went to first base as the Pirates took the field for the ninth inning. The token appearance allowed Musial to establish a league record of having played in 895 consecutive games. He officially played his 895th consecutive game five days earlier, on August 22, in Philadelphia. During that game, Musial pulled a

muscle in his left shoulder and hadn't played until his
appearance at the resumed game.

5. *Sports Illustrated,* July 29, 1957, p. 5. The reference by
Sports Illustrated to the Dodgers having won nine out
of eleven games (instead of ten out of twelve) during
this period would indicate that the magazine went to
press after the first game of the Dodgers-Cubs doubleheader of July 21 but before the second game was completed.

6. In addition to the moniker "Toothpick," Jones had the
distinction of owning a second nickname. No one could
blame "Sad" Sam Jones for feeling down after this loss.

Chapter 6

An Indelible Memory

What a ball game the Dodgers and the Cardinals played on July 18! *The Sporting News* called the ninth inning "[the] most fantastic inning of [the] season,"[1] and I had seen my hero on the Dodgers, Duke Snider, hit a home run and score the winning run. Despite its roller coaster excitement and sudden death finish, the Dodger victory competed for headlines with another ball game and, together, they represented a turning point in the 1957 National League pennant race. Eighty miles southwest of Ebbets Field, at Connie Mack Stadium in Philadelphia, the Braves completed a three-game sweep against the Phillies and moved into first place. It was the fourth time in five days that first place had changed hands but with the outcome of the Brooklyn and Philadelphia contests on July 18, the National League standings came into alignment with the rankings that would exist at the end of the year: Milwaukee first, St. Louis second, and Brooklyn third.

Milwaukee was the sleeping giant of the first half of the 1957 season. With its 5-2 loss to the seventh-place Pirates on July 10, Milwaukee trailed first-place St. Louis by three games. The turnaround in Milwaukee's fortunes began the next day, July 11, which was the same day when the Dodgers mounted their own mid-season pennant drive. The Braves defeated the Pirates 7-2 and went on to post a 10-3 record during July 11-23. It could have been a very different story. Coming off a 20-4 drubbing at the hands of the Dodgers on July 15 and facing a three-game series against the suddenly first-place Phillies on their home turf in Philadelphia, the Braves might have gone into a tailspin from which they couldn't recover. Instead it was the Phillies who would suffer that fate.

Milwaukee's performance improved as its list of injured players increased almost daily. An article by Bob Wolf in *The Sporting News* was prophetic. Carrying the headline "Braves Beaming Despite Rash of Aches n' Breaks," it read:

> When the crippled Braves limped
> home [to Milwaukee on July 23] from
> their third eastern trip in first place, they
> felt confident that they had taken their
> biggest stride yet toward the National
> League pennant. If they could win . . .
> with a patched-up lineup, they reasoned,
> how could anybody stop them once they
> got their strength back?[2]

Wolf pointed to the man, Red Schoendienst, whose hitting and fielding were holding Milwaukee together: "The Redhead hit .368 on the eastern trip, fielded like a magician at second base and generally made the [June 1957] trade which brought him to the Braves from the Giants look better than ever."[3] Declared Wolf: "[Schoendienst's] magnificent work at second had been one of the big reasons for the club's rise to the top of the league."[4]

Milwaukee finished second to Brooklyn in 1953 and 1955, and in 1956 they lost the pennant by a single game on the last day of the season, posting a 92-62 record to the Dodgers' 93 wins and 61 losses. In a pre-season article the following spring, the Associated Press (AP) reported that "many think Milwaukee has developed a 'second place complex'."[5] In 1957 Milwaukee would not be denied. From a 44-35 record on July 10, the Braves would go on to win 51 games and lose 24, to end the year with a pennant-winning 95-59 record

On the eve of baseball's opening day in 1957, the AP wrote: "All observers expect another tight race in the National League. . . . The Dodgers and Braves, co-favorites, probably will fight it out again, with Cincinnati also challenging. A long distant threat from St. Louis . . . just about sums up the National."[6] The Dodgers fell well short of that prediction during the first half of the season, with their fifth place position and 41-36 record. This was followed, however, by the Dodgers' post-All Star game surge in the standings, which was the most exciting period of their last year in Brooklyn.

Some histories of the Dodgers have overlooked this part of the story. One account states: "What the [Dodger] team did in its final year at Ebbets Field left nothing to be remembered."[7] Another flatly asserts: "In 1957 they [the Dodgers] were never in the pennant race."[8] In fact, the Dodgers' five-game winning streak of July 11-16 brought them back into solid pennant contention, going from fifth place, five games out of first, to fourth place, one game out. The victories of July 18-19 raised Brooklyn from fourth place, one-and-a-half games out of first, to second place, one game out. On July 20, 21, and 23, the Dodgers would have taken over first place if Milwaukee had lost on any of those days, including both games of their July 21st doubleheader.

Roscoe McGowen wrote about the man, Duke Snider, whose performance did the most to spark the Dodgers' pennant drive:

> When the Dodgers were in the midst
> of their highly successful home stand . . .
> Walt Alston made the comment: "When
> Snider hits, we win."

> Snider belted eight home runs . . . . He
> batted in 15 runs, scored 14 and drew 13
> bases on balls.
> Besides his homers, the Duke smacked
> seven other hits, including one double,
> giving him a batting average . . . of .385.[9]

The Dodgers' 11-2 record during July 11-23 gave Brooklyn fans hope for one more pennant. In the end, it accounted only for the Dodgers' marginally better perform- ance, 43-34, during the second half of the season. On July 24-25 the Dodgers lost the last two games of their three- game series in St. Louis, yielding second place to the Cardinals on July 25. Brooklyn ended the year with an 84- 70 record, three games behind St. Louis and eleven games behind Milwaukee.[10]

By mid-July 1957, news about the Dodgers' fortunes on the ball field was starting to contend for space in the sports pages with an ominous development for Brooklyn fans: the increasing likelihood that their beloved team would not be around the following year.

Among those attending the Dodgers-Braves game at Ebbets Field on July 14 was Lou Perini, the president and chief owner of the Milwaukee Braves. In remarks to the press that day, Perini predicted that the Dodgers would leave Ebbets Field. Referring to Walter O'Malley, the president of the Brooklyn Dodgers, he said: "O'Malley can't live here. But whether he'll move to Los Angeles or some other location I wouldn't say."[11]

O'Malley had frequently stated that Ebbets Field was antiquated, did not have sufficient or desirable seats, and, above all, had extremely limited parking facilities. He wanted a new ball park. Indeed, thanks to O'Malley, the Dodgers were already tenants in their own home. On

Dodger president Walter O'Malley peers through the plastic cover of a proposed new field.

Source: *Sports Illustrated.*

October 30, 1956 he sold Ebbets Field for $3 million to a real estate operator, Marvin Kratter, who planned to construct a $25 million residential and commercial development on the site. The contract that was signed that day allowed the Dodgers to continue to play at Ebbets Field until the end of the 1959 season under a lease, with an option to extend this arrangement through 1961 at a higher figure.

O'Malley faced no jurisdictional obstacles if he chose to move to the west coast. At a special meeting in Chicago on May 28, 1957, National League directors gave their permission for the Dodgers and the New York Giants to request consent before October 1 to relocate their franchises to Los Angeles and San Francisco, respectively. The league specified that it must be a "package deal."[12] One club could not move without the other.

An alternative was for the Dodgers to build a new facility in Brooklyn or elsewhere in the New York City area. Addressing himself to that possibility, Perini observed: "Maybe the Dodgers could land at another location nearby. I'll tell you, I'd like to see [New York Park Commissioner Robert] Moses build that park at the Flushing site he's been talking about. He'd have everything there – parking and a lot of other things."[13]

On July 15 the new issue of *Sports Illustrated* carried a lengthy article by Moses. It was entitled "Robert Moses on the Battle of Brooklyn: New York's Outspoken Park Commissioner, Accusing the Dodgers' O'Malley of Bad Faith, Presents a Plan for a National League Site in N.Y."[14]

Moses recalled O'Malley's long-standing dissatisfaction with Ebbets Field along with the ball park's sale and lease arrangement, then added:

> This news was accompanied by heart-rending appeals [by O'Malley] not to leave Brooklyn flat. Walter then memorized a speech indicating that he would die for dear old Brooklyn. He also announced that he would at least postpone a decision while he and other simple, open-handed, guileless business-men waited for scheming politicians to

The caption to this photo read: "Uncompromising Robert Moses puts on fighting face that has become famous."

Source: *Sports Illustrated.*

build him a new field. I have heard this
speech over and over again *ad nauseam*.[15]

According to Moses, O'Malley had originally asked that
part of the Brooklyn civic center be turned over to him.
When rebuffed, he shifted his interest to the Long Island
Rail Road terminal at Atlantic Avenue in Brooklyn. Moses
addressed the possibility of a new stadium at this location:
"Let me now in my own words give you briefly what I
believe will be the conclusions as to the Atlantic terminal
site. It won't happen."[16] He cited lack of time and finan-
cial considerations as the primary obstacles.

Moses went on to plug what in his judgment was "the
only suggestion involving park land which makes any

sense,"[17] namely an all-purpose municipal stadium and sports center that would be located in Flushing Meadow Park. Its location, however, was in Queens, not Brooklyn, and Moses conceded that "its locale was . . . a fatal defect from the point of view of some Brooklyn fanatics."[18] It was also a plan that had been laid out on paper by the Park Department twenty years earlier but had never come to fruition.

In the end, were the Dodgers and the Giants going to stay in New York or leave for the west coast? Moses wrote:

> It was accepted as gospel that if the
> Dodgers left Ebbets Field in Brooklyn
> the Giants would leave the Polo Grounds
> in Manhattan, and thus New York would
> have no National League team at all –
> only the Yankees in the American League.
> I am unable to explain the logic of such
> an exodus of all National League players,
> but smarter people than I have stated that
> it is inevitable. . . . Whether either team
> has actually signed up to go, I don't
> know. They have received permission,
> conditionally, from the other National
> League clubs to move. From my seat in
> the bleachers *it looks as if the Dodgers
> at least are already on the way* [italics
> added].[19]

On July 18 Moses' article in *Sports Illustrated* made news when *The New York Times* ran a story on it under the headline "Moses Denounces O'Malley Tactics."[20] The newspaper quoted several of Moses' remarks about O'Malley and reported on the Dodger president's response to the article in which he charged that Moses "is speaking only for Moses"[21] and not for other New York City officials, including Brooklyn Sports Center Authority Chairman Charles J. Mylod, Brooklyn Borough President John Cashmore, and Mayor Robert F. Wagner.

Amidst the war of words, a billboard in Brooklyn was scheduled to begin carrying a message that week at the intersection of Washington Avenue and Sullivan Place, three blocks from Ebbets Field. Paid for by a Los Angeles advertising agency, it wished the Dodgers good luck in Brooklyn "until next year in Los Angeles."[22] Most of the management and workers of the Brooklyn billboard company that was to do the job were fans of the Dodgers. They refused to erect the billboard.

On October 7 the Los Angeles City Council voted 10-4 to approve an ordinance embodying the terms of a contract that was previously agreed upon with executives of the Brooklyn Dodgers. It would make Chavez Ravine, located on the edge of downtown Los Angeles, available for the multimillion dollar, ultramodern stadium that Walter O'Malley intended to build there. The ordinance was officially signed that evening by Los Angeles Mayor Norris Poulson.

At 4:00 P.M. the next day, representatives for both the Brooklyn Dodgers and the National League gathered in the World Series pressroom of the Waldorf-Astoria Hotel in New York City. Walter O'Malley was not present but he issued a statement that was read to assembled baseball reporters by Arthur "Red" Patterson, the assistant general manager and publicity man for the Dodgers. The terse announcement said:

> In view of the action of the Los
> Angeles City Council yesterday and in

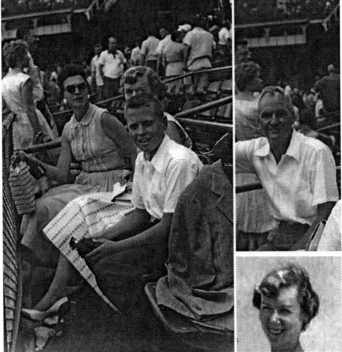

(Top) The Nordell family watches Duke Snider's climactic dash for home.

Source: *Daily News* (New York).

(Bottom) After the game, the author sits with his mother (left), aunt (partially concealed and bottom right), and father (top right).

accordance with the resolution of the
National League made Oct. 1 [to extend
the deadline for a decision], the stock-
holders and directors of the Brooklyn
Baseball Club have today met and
unanimously agreed that necessary steps
be taken to draft the Los Angeles
territory [for 1958].[23]

The official end of the Dodgers in Brooklyn came only
eighty-two days after the game between the Dodgers and
the Cardinals that my family and I watched at Ebbets Field
on July 18. With the O'Malley statement, however, that
game had become part of another era.

I am grateful that we saw the Dodgers play in Brooklyn
before the opportunity vanished forever. On that unforget-
table day we watched a mid-summer afternoon baseball
game in an intimate baseball park that new stadiums some-
times try to imitate but will never duplicate. I saw my
team – the amazing Brooklyn Dodgers – stage a dramatic
come-from-behind victory while in the thick of a five-team
pennant race. Subsequent events, however disappointing,
could never diminish that indelible memory. It is the
memory of a lifetime.

Notes to Chapter 6

1. *The Sporting News,* July 31, 1957, p. 23.

2. Ibid., p. 11.

3. Ibid.

4. Ibid.

5. *The Wilkes-Barre Record,* April 8, 1957, p. 11.

6. *The Wilkes-Barre Record,* April 15, 1957, p. 13. In 1956 the Cincinnati Redlegs had a 91-63 record and finished the season in third place, one game behind the Braves and two games behind the Dodgers. The St. Louis Cardinals finished in fourth place, with a 76-78 record.

7. Tommy Holmes, *The Dodgers,* p. 121.

8. Glenn Stout, *The Dodgers: 120 Years of Dodgers Baseball,* p. 238.

9. *The Sporting News,* July 31, 1957, p. 15.

10. See the appendix for the final National League standings in 1957.

11. *The New York Times,* July 15, 1957, p. 23.

12. *The Wilkes-Barre Record,* May 29, 1957, p. 18.

13. *The New York Times,* July 15, 1957, p. 23.

14. *Sports Illustrated,* July 22, 1957, pp. 26-27.

15. Ibid.

16. Ibid., p. 46.

17. Ibid., p. 48.

18. Ibid.

19. Ibid., p. 28.

20. *The New York Times,* July 18, 1957, p. 51.

21. Ibid.

22. Bob McGee, *The Greatest Ballpark Ever: Ebbets Field and the Story of the Brooklyn Dodgers,* p. 269.

23. *The New York Times,* October 9, 1957, p. 37. On August 19, 1957 the New York Giants' board of directors voted to shift their franchise to San Francisco in 1958. Giant president Horace Stoneham made the announcement to a gathering of reporters and photographers at the Giants' offices in New York.

Appendix

Standings	Won	Lost	Pct.	GB
Milwaukee Braves	95	59	.617	-
St. Louis Cardinals	87	67	.565	8
Brooklyn Dodgers	84	70	.545	11
Cincinnati Redlegs	80	74	.519	15
Philadelphia Phillies	77	77	.500	18
New York Giants	69	85	.448	26
Pittsburgh Pirates	62	92	.403	33
Chicago Cubs	62	92	.403	33

Bibliography

Newspapers, Magazines, and Wire Services

Associated Press

Daily News (New York)

News Colorfotos

Newsweek

New York Times

1957 Dodger yearbook

1958 Dodger yearbook

1958 Who's Who in Sports

Sporting News

Sports Illustrated

Street & Smith's 1958 Baseball Yearbook

Time

Wilkes-Barre Record

Books

Holmes, Tommy. *The Dodgers.* New York: Macmillan
Publishing Company, Inc., 1975.

McGee, Bob. *The Greatest Ballpark Ever: Ebbets Field
and the Story of the Brooklyn Dodgers.* New
Brunswick, New Jersey: Rutgers University Press,
2005.

Rice, Damon. *Seasons Past.* New York: Praeger
Publishers, Inc., 1976.

Roeder, Bill, "(Gil Hodges) The Strong Man," in Tom
Meany et. al., *The Artful Dodgers,* rev. New York:
Grosset & Dunlap, 1958.

Stout, Glenn. *The Dodgers: 120 Years of Dodgers
Baseball.* Boston: Houghton Mifflin Company, 2004.

Audio Recordings

Major League Baseball, The Miley Collection, Brooklyn
vs. Milwaukee, July 14, 1957.

Major League Baseball, The Miley Collection, Brooklyn
vs. Chicago, July 20, 1957.

Internet

www.retrosheet.org.

Index

Printed in the United States
89936LV00001B/1-99/A